5
95

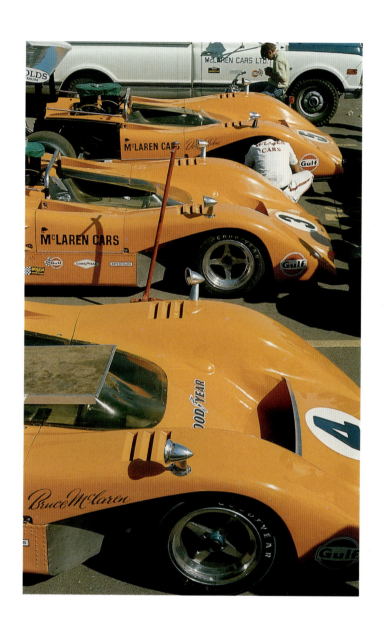

CAN-AM
PHOTO HISTORY

Pete Lyons

MBI Publishing Company

First published in 1999 by MBI Publishing Company, 729 Prospect Avenue, PO Box 1, Osceola, WI 54020-0001 USA

© Pete Lyons, 1999

All rights reserved. With the exception of quoting brief passages for the purpose of review no part of this publication may be reproduced without prior written permission from the Publisher.

The information in this book is true and complete to the best of our knowledge. All recommendations are made without any guarantee on the part of the author or Publisher, who also disclaim any liability incurred in connection with the use of this data or specific details.

No part of this book may be reproduced without expressed, written permission from the publisher. For information about permission to reproduce selections from this book, write to: 729 Prospect Avenue, PO Box 1, Osceola, WI 54020-0001 USA

We recognize that some words, model names, and designations mentioned in this book are the property of the trademark holder. We use them only for identification purposes.

MBI Publishing Company books are also available at discounts in bulk quantity for industrial or sales-promotional use. For details write to Special Sales Manager at Motorbooks International Wholesalers & Distributors, 729 Prospect Avenue, PO Box 1, Osceola, WI 54020-0001 USA.

Library of Congress Cataloging-in-Publication Data Available

ISBN 0-7603-0806-3

On the front cover: Jim Hall and his Chaparral 2G, Riverside 1968. No cars better illustrate the meaning of the grand old "unlimited" Can-Am than Hall's incredibly innovative Road Runners from Texas. *Pete Lyons*

On the frontispiece: Team McLaren, Laguna Seca 1969. The Can-Am's longest season was also the greatest for Bruce McLaren and Denny Hulme. The Kiwis were the only team to win that year (and the only one with a spare car). *Pete Lyons*

On the title page: Penske's Porsche Panzers, Donnybrooke 1972. Shaking the earth with almost 1,000 horsepower, the German factory's turbocharged engines were the first to win in road racing—and the first to push the once-invincible McLaren-Chevrolets into obscurity. *Pete Lyons*

On the back cover, Top: Mark Donohue, America's most successful Can-Am driver with nine career victories, and team owner Roger Penske struggled with older cars, such as this painstakingly modified 1968 McLaren M6B, before joining forces with Porsche to beat McLaren at its own game. *Pete Lyons Bottom:* Though the cars were the stars, the Can-Am was actually a driver's championship and it showcased the world's best. Here, from left, are "Champagne Peter" Revson, "the Mod Scot" Jackie Stewart, and Denny "the Bear" Hulme. *Pete Biro*

Edited by Paul Johnson
Designed by Rebecca Allen

Printed in China

Contents

	Acknowledgments	7
Introduction	**1966 to 1974: The Age of Thunder** **The Canadian-American Challenge Cup**	9
Chapter 1	**1966: Wild, Winged, Wonderful** **Can-Am's Glorious Debut**	27
Chapter 2	**1967: Kiwi Domination** **Bruce and Denny Play America**	57
Chapter 3	**1968: Bigger Bangers** **The Teams Embrace Big Block Power**	79
Chapter 4	**1969: Bruce, Denny, Bruce, Denny . . .** **McLaren's Greatest Season**	101
Chapter 5	**1970: A New Era** **Can-Am Goes Conventional**	119
Chapter 6	**1971: Stewart and Lola Challenge McLaren** **McLaren's Peter Revson Takes the Crown**	135
Chapter 7	**1972: Big Blown Banger** **The Dawn of the Porsche Era**	151
Chapter 8	**1973: Porsche Perfect** **Penske's Panzer Thoroughly Dominates**	163
Chapter 9	**1974: Long Shadows** **The Curtain Closes on the Can-Am**	175
Appendix	**Can-Am Year-By-Year Results**	183
	Index	191

Acknowledgments

Having already done it once, I had the idea that getting through a second book on the old Canadian-American Challenge Cup series—a seemingly simple followup to 1995's *Can-Am* (also published by MBI Publishing Company)—would be quick and easy. That idea was as foolish as expecting one's next race to go smoothly. Many blown pistons, stripped gears, and broken good intentions later, here it comes at long last, still shedding bits of shattered deadlines, and trailing smoke from the publisher's phone calls.

But, as does any worn-out, beat-up, overheated driver who hopes to drive again, before heading for the shower and the party, I must effusively express my gratitude to everybody who helped.

As always, writ largest on my metaphorical race car is the name of my marvelous wife, Lorna. Her patience and encouragement were as helpful as her orderly and positive mind. Thank you, Sweetheart.

Powering this project were the former Can-Am racers of the great unlimited era who so generously contributed their personal recollections: Tyler Alexander, Mario Andretti, Peter Bryant, George Follmer, Dan Gurney, Jim Hall, Phil Hill, Denny Hulme, Parnelli Jones, Teddy Mayer, Bob McKee, Jackie Oliver, Alwin Springer, and John Surtees. Needless to say, many other important Can-Am history-makers deserved to be included. I apologize to the many I've missed, and also to those who sat for my tape recorder, but whose words I couldn't manage to pack in. Unfortunately, unlike them, I can't handle an unlimited amount of horsepower.

Equally, I am deeply grateful to the photographers and/or photo sources who contributed many more great images than it was possible to include. Those whose fine work survived the painful final cut were Tyler Alexander through the courtesy of Ron Hussey, *Autosport* magazine, Lionel Birnbom, Pete Biro, Jim Chambers, Joanne Dearcopp, Ray Jeanotte, Harry Kennison, Daniel Lipetz, my sister Claire Lyons McHenry, my father Ozzie Lyons, Rich Mitter, Bill Oursler, John Rettie, Joe Rusz of *Road & Track* magazine, Bob Tronolone, Dale von Trebra, Bill Warner, and Ben Williams courtesy of Michael Recca.

While most of this material is published here for the first time, certain passages and photographs have appeared previously in various magazines. My grateful acknowledgment goes to the editors and staff of *Autosport, AutoWeek, Racer, Road & Track, Vintage Motorsport,* and *Vintage Racecar Journal & Market Report.*

As with the 1995 book, David Hahs must be recognized for his superb photo printing skills and devotion to perfection.

I owe another special thank you to the late Canadian historian Doug Waters. He personally filled in many blanks in my own knowledge, while his painstakingly compiled Can-Am marque and event documentation—made available through the kindness of Randy Leffingwell—was invaluable.

Similarly, I'm indebted to the numerous readers of *Can-Am* who have taken the trouble over the past four years to illuminate points I left obscure, or to set me straight where I erred. I can only hope I've cut a cleaner lap this time.

Of course, this book would not have happened at all without the commitment of Tim Parker, Zack Miller, and Paul Johnson of MBI Publishing Company. Thanks for keeping my foot on the gas, guys.

In closing, I wish to dedicate this book in loving memory to Lisa McHenry.

—*Pete Lyons, Big Bear, California*

Introduction

1966 to 1974: The Age of Thunder

The Canadian-American Challenge Cup

"At the time, it was just Bruce and me and the team having a good time. What I didn't realize, and I'm only beginning to work it out . . . I was part of a very historic piece of motor racing in the United States."

Denis Hulme said that in 1990, during a Can-Am reunion at Watkins Glen. I believe he was speaking for every fan there. He sure spoke for me.

Denny-the-Bear, King of the Can-Am, was twice the series champion and won more of its races than anyone else—more than twice as many. A man big in both body and heart, he stamped his own sturdy soul deep into that brawny era. Hulme also won Formula One's World Driving Championship in 1967, but if this New Zealander seemed born to one thing, it was North America's "unlimited" Canadian-American Challenge Cup sports car spectacle from 1966 through 1974.

Those were years when race cars shook the earth, when engines bellowed free of limits, and the machines they powered were the wildest road racers on earth. The Can-Am was a child of the Psychedelic 1960s, launched along with rockets to the moon and revolutions in society. American racing's great technological adventure was a noble experiment in unchained performance.

When the old, original Can-Am was alive, everything about it was big—cars, stars, dollars. At the beginning, Can-Am cars had 500 horsepower and could beat Formula One cars around a Grand Prix circuit. Before the end, there were 1,200-horsepower engines and straightaway speeds that potentially could top 240 miles per hour—astounding numbers in those days.

To be precise, the "unlimited" Can-Am wasn't quite that. Cars had to be two-seaters with bodywork covering all wheels and "coachwork" incorporating cockpit doors. Fuel was supposed to be straight gasoline, and of course there were certain safety requirements. In later years so-called "moving aerodynamic devices" were banned, and just before the end, a cap was put on fuel consumption.

But in most ways the old Can-Am car remained gloriously free. Engine design and displacement—even the number of engines per car—were always open, and so were vehicle dimensions, configurations, materials. Tires could be as big and grippy as Goodyear or Firestone cared to make them. There was never a weight minimum.

Unlimited engines called forth unlimited technologies. Wings on race cars were first established in the Can-Am, and so were aerodynamic ground effects, and turbochargers, too. In fact, North America's free-formula sports car racing gave birth to many innovations later outlawed as too radical.

The old Can-Am was natural soil for Chaparral, that hothouse of innovation. It was a wellspring of practical performance for McLaren. Porsche made its mighty "Panzer" for the Can-Am. Secret Chevrolets, fabulous Fords, frenetic Ferraris,

New series, new ideas: at Bridgehampton 1966, the wild, winged Road Runner (No. 65 Phil Hill, Chaparral 2E) towers above the Lolas and McLarens of the day. It was the only design that year to stretch the conventional concept of the Can-Am car. *Pete Biro*

Stacked: Tall, staggered-length intake trumpets atop unlimited Reynolds-block Chevrolet engines, such McLaren's at Mosport in 1971, became the old Can-Am's signature icon. *Pete Lyons*

Wings over Riverside: By 1969 nearly every front-line Can-Am car wore the high, suspension-mounted airfoils invented by Chaparral three years earlier. By 1970 this innovation was banned, sending the once wide-open series down a road of ever-tightening restrictions. *Pete Lyons*

Can-Am Fans: In 1970 the Chaparral 2J, a.k.a. Chevrolet Ground Effect Vehicle, used a pair of extractor fans powered by a separate engine and sliding Lexan skirts to create downforce with low drag everywhere around the track. Vic Elford drove the "Sucker" to fastest qualifying lap here at Laguna Seca and at other tracks. *Bob Tronolone*

lovely Lolas, startling Shadows, the tidy "Titanium Car," the weird little *Mac's-It Special* with four engines—there was always something marvelous at a Can-Am.

People, too. Actually a driver's championship, the Can-Am had the world's best. Many came from the Formula One and Indy car ranks, drawn by the most lavish purse structure their sport had ever seen. The Can-Am grew to be a "Million-Dollar" spectacle at a time when such a value commanded awe.

Bruce McLaren, Jim Hall, and Mark Donohue were Can-Am drivers. There was Big George Follmer, Bigger Dan Gurney, and Fearless John Surtees, Wee Jackie Stewart, Champagne Peter Revson, and The Bear—Denny Hulme. In fact, almost any great road racer of the era you could name tried his hand at the "Big Bangers."

The Can-Am also gave free license to some of the sport's greatest designers, crew chiefs, mechanics, technicians, and craftsmen. The series visited most of this continent's finest road courses.

Winged Road Runner: "I'm probably more responsible for downforce on race cars than anybody I know of," says Chaparral founder Jim Hall. The "flipper" he patented with Chevrolet engineers in 1966 let Road Runner drivers push a pedal to flatten the wing for reduced air drag on straightaways. Hall demonstrates at Bridgehampton in 1968, where he led the race for five laps with his 2G. *Pete Lyons*

As a race-rabid young journalist, I followed six full seasons of the Can-Am for England's *Autosport* magazine, so the series was seminal in my career. Besides, I loved those cars, those people, and those times for their own sakes. *Can-Am*, published by MBI Publishing Co. in 1995, was a labor of that love. The first complete record of the series, it was necessarily a blow-by-blow historical account.

In *Can-Am Memories: A Photohistory*, we take a more reflective look at the same nine-year period. There is some straight history to provide context, but the bulk of the words are those of the racers themselves, looking back. We also focus on some of the cars in greater detail. All the photos are new, most published here for the first time.

As was the first book, this one is devoted to the first Can-Am period of 1966–74. Several

Weird Science: The freewheeling Can-Am encouraged such startling experiments as Advanced Vehicle Systems (AVS) *Tiny Tire* Shadow, which sought low drag with super small Firestones. Rolling out their Roller Skate at Mosport in 1970 are team leader Don Nichols (left) and designer Trevor Harris (far right). The giant, conventional vehicle in the foreground is the Ti22 Titanium Car, built by Peter Bryant, who joined Shadow a year later. *Pete Lyons*

Porsche Panzer: Many road racers had tried turbocharging, but the first team to make it work right was the German automaker and Penske's American driver-engineer Mark Donohue. Able to develop in excess of 950 horsepower, 200 more than contemporary Chevy V-8s, the twin-turbo, 12-cylinder Porsche 917/10K ousted long-dominant McLaren from the Can-Am in 1972. Donohue, seen powersliding the Laguna Seca hairpin here, missed too many races that year to be champion but would make up for it in 1973. *Pete Lyons*

Supercar: Disappointed with his 1972 season, Mark Donohue came back the next year with a totally revamped Porsche. The 917/30 had a larger, 5.4-liter engine rated at 1,190 horsepower, though it was capable of pumping out over 1,500. To handle all that, the car had a longer wheelbase, stiffer chassis frame, revised suspension geometry, and refined aerodynamics. It really wasn't fair to the other guys—which was exactly what Mark intended. *Daniel Lipetz*

subsequent racing formulae have carried the name, but their stories don't belong here.

Why was the old, original Canadian-American Challenge Cup so special? Fair question. After all this time, one thing everyone remembers about the Can-Am was the rap against it for "boring racing." Though there were some good moments, especially during the inaugural 1966 season, let's face it, most of the old Can-Ams weren't even close. Bruce McLaren seized the series as his own in 1967, and either he or Hulme won most of the races and all of the championships for four consecutive years. In 1969, they won every race of the Can-Am's longest season—11 straight. Even those of us who loved it called it "The Bruce and Denny Show."

We lost Bruce McLaren in 1970, killed while testing a new car, but the team he founded steamrollered on through 1971. In all, cars built by McLaren won 43 of the 71 races held in the old series. In those nine years, Team McLaren drivers McLaren, Hulme, and Revson took five Can-Am championships.

Then, once Porsche emerged as an effective challenger in 1972, it quickly gained dominance. One show was replaced with another even more predictable. Turbo-Porsches placed first 14 times in the 17 races of 1972 and 1973, with factory

A Rare Real Race: Most of the time Can-Am enthusiasts had to be content with watching great cars, but occasionally they got some great track action. At Mosport in 1970, Dan Gurney (No. 48 McLaren M8D) had to chase Jackie Oliver (No. 22 Bryant Ti22, partly obscured) through the pack (No. 24 Bob Nagle, Lola T70, and No. 51 Dave Causey, Lola T163) to victory, keeping the McLaren dynasty going. *Pete Lyons*

drivers George Follmer and Mark Donohue winning those year's titles. McLaren didn't even try that second year.

For 1974 Porsche dropped out. Shadow took over. The "Shadow Show" was as good as one two-car team could make it, but it wasn't good enough to save the series. After just five races,

Press facilities, 1960s style: Journalist Christine Laidlaw pounds out her story at Quebec's St. Jovite, 1969. *Pete Lyons*

The mile-long straight: Everybody tried to bring their strongest engines to Riverside for the wide, downhill run back toward the pits. We can see how they did in 1968 as early as Lap 1: braking hard into the banked Turn 9 are McLaren and Hulme (McLaren M8As), Donohue (M6B) and Hall (Chaparral 2G), that year's main players. *Pete Lyons*

Will race for fun: Oscar Koveleski, owner of the No. 54 AutoWorld McLaren, was one Can-Am driver who had as good a time off-track as on it. *Ray Jeanotte*

Racer relations: In those relaxed days before media managers and motor homes, drivers like Bruce McLaren got to do their own PR up close and personal, as here at St. Jovite in 1969. *Pete Lyons*

California dreamin': Before the 1969 season, not even that sunny optimist Bruce McLaren would have expected his team's high-winged M8Bs to romp to victory in all 11 races. He himself scored six times—this, at California's Laguna Seca, was No. 5—and took his second driver's championship. *Pete Lyons*

Bruce and Denny Show: Ambition, dedication, single-minded practicality and solid hard driving earned New Zealanders Bruce McLaren (left) and 1967 World Champion Denis Hulme the Can-Am's "Floatile" Johnson Wax trophy year after year. *Lionel Birnbom*

the Can-Am died. So the racing was generally dull, and so were the cars, at least for some people. Indeed, they were bulky, ungainly sports models lacking the delicate grace of contemporary open-wheelers. They had more bodywork and more seats than necessary for a competition instrument. More engine, too; it was all brute force, critics sniffed, lacking the sophisticated driving challenge posed by lightweight single-seaters. Nor were those engines, which were pushrod Detroit V-8s, truly pure of blood.

Ah, but you could feel those big blocks shake the ground. They really did. And you could go to the next race confident of seeing something new. We usually did. Best of all, you could catch a ride in a Can-Am car. I did.

And there was some good racing—some terrific racing. In the end, the biggest thing about the big-bang, big-buck Can-Am is that it made road racing important in America. As Denny said, it was historic.

Engines Unlimited

In the beginning, the state-of-the-Can-Am-art was a small block, all-iron Chevy stroked to as much as six liters and breathing through a quartet of twin-barrel Weber carbs. That gave drivers such as Jerry Grant, whose Lola T70 lies in wait for him at Bridgehampton 1966, upward of 500 horsepower. *Pete Lyons*

UNLIMITED. In the old Can-Am that word could have meant body shapes, or drive systems, or almost anything else, but we all know it really meant . . . horsepower! Going from fewer than 500 ponies at the start of the series to over 1,000 Percherons before the end, powerplants made rapid progress, and forced all other automotive technologies to keep up. Hot rodders built the first Can-Am race motors out of discarded passenger car parts. Soon auto factories began contributing new, special hardware along with scientific expertise, but for several seasons each team was responsible for doing its own tuning and maintenance, or having it done. That era came to an end when Porsche conquered the problems of turbocharging, and supplied its 917 car as a complete package.

Beginning in 1968, McLaren made the big aluminum Chevrolet the performance icon of the age. *Harry Kennison*

Ford's only successful Can-Am driver was Dan Gurney, who put his own Weslake-designed aluminum heads on Dearborn's smallest iron block and scored a 1966 victory. Dan kept trying the same prescription for several more years (pictured is his 1967 unit, distinguished from the earlier version by nonvertical fuel injection intakes), but without further luck. *Pete Lyons*

Parnelli Jones and Mario Andretti took Ford's exotic DOHC Indianapolis engine into sports car war during 1967 and 1968. *Pete Lyons*

Peter Revson drove this 427 with crossover stacks for Carroll Shelby early in 1968. *Pete Lyons*

Engines

Later, Shelby replaced the cross-over inlet design with this verticle offset configuration. *Pete Lyons*

Though called the "429er," the engine behind Andretti in 1969 was a hemi-head monster displacing 494 ci. Mario said the acceleration was so strong he couldn't reach forward to shift. *Pete Lyons*

Charlie and Kerry Agapiou later race-tested the 494 with a different injection and exhaust configuration. Their chassis was an aging, former Le Mans model that Ford once meant to race itself, but never did. *Pete Lyons*

Above, right, and facing page: Individual tuning firms like Bartz and Traco were working out their own solutions to the Big Bow Tie's troubles. Externally obvious variations were in the areas of intake stack length, injector and throttle valve positioning, and routing of passages to cool the fuel. *Pete Lyons*

Engines

Left and top: In 1967 Chevrolet gave its aluminum 427 to Chaparral for early race-testing. It needed a lot of that. *Pete Lyons*

The Chaparral team's work resulted in a reliable aluminum 427 Chevy used by most of the privateer racers. *Pete Lyons*

Engines

The well-connected Kiwis stayed on the Chevrolet corporate ladder, continuing to use the factory heads and getting first use of the sleeveless Reynolds blocks in 1970. In 1972, at Riverside, they punched one out to over 9.25 liters for Hulme's last try at pole. *Pete Lyons*

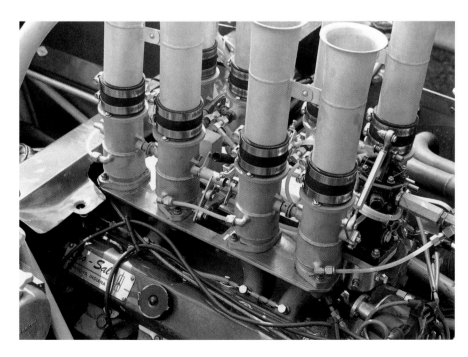

Bucking the tide toward Chevrolet, Gene Crowe (of Cro-Sal) kept the Oldsmobile faith. This is one of his bigger ones of 1968, but not yet the turbocharged model he was the first to race a year later. *Pete Lyons*

Ferrari's 6.2-liter V-12 of 1969 was a gorgeous thing to behold. It was almost fast enough—when it lasted. *Pete Lyons*

Engines

Porsche's solution to the Can-Am power problem was a turbocharged 12. Not the first turbo in road racing, but the first to work well, the quad-cam motor was massive and complex. In addition to a wastegate (not installed on the engines pictured), it had a pair of small, downward pointing inlets linked to the throttle mechanism, apparently to smooth low-speed response. In the first year, there were also eight independent, spring-loaded inlets atop the intake "logs." Those were gone from the 1973 version. *Pete Lyons/Bob Tronolone*

In a brave effort to beat Porsche at the turbo game, Shadow spent two years trying to boost its Chevy engines to the front. As here in 1972, it logged a lot of garage time. *Pete Lyons*

Another turbo Chevy was the bristling 1973 monster that frightened Mario Andretti's mechanic speechless. But ain't it purty? *Pete Lyons*

25

1966: Wild, Winged, Wonderful

Can-Am's Glorious Debut

The Canadian-American Challenge Cup series was designed around the international Grand Prix calendar, in hopes of attracting Formula One drivers. Sure enough, three of them gave the new sports car show a rousing debut. On the beautiful "Le Circuit" at Quebec's Mt. Tremblant-St. Jovite, former World Champion John Surtees (Lola-Chevy) raced hard for over two hours, six minutes to scratch out a 6.5-second victory from Bruce McLaren (McLaren-Chevy).

It might have been closer, but in the last laps they were split by McLaren's teammate Chris Amon. Chrissy, the brilliant young New Zealander, lost a lap and a half in the pits and then set records—beating Surtees' pole position speed—catching up and trying to pass Surtees to get back on the same lap. Surtees felt it was safer not to let him.

The original starting field boasted 34 names, including Dan Gurney, Parnelli Jones, George Follmer, Jerry Grant, Ron Bucknum, Mark Donohue, Chuck Parsons, Masten Gregory, Skip Scott, John Cannon, Sam Posey, Ludwig Heimrath, Lothar Motschenbacher, Charlie Hayes, and Eppie Wietzes. And the crowd was the track's biggest ever. So the Can-Am looked like an instant hit.

However, drivers of these big, powerful, wide-body racers left St. Jovite in a thoughtful mood. Two of them, Paul Hawkins and Hugh Dibley, had somehow survived "blow-overs" during practice, when their aerodynamic-looking Lola T70s lifted off like airplanes over a hump in a high-speed straightaway and flipped right

Phil Hill (#65 Chaparral 2E), America's 1961 Formula One World Driving Champion, leads teammate Jim Hall to the innovative marque's only Can-Am victory at Laguna Seca in 1966. Splitting the winged Road Runners through the famous Corkscrew turn is Bruce McLaren (#4 McLaren M1B), whose own name would become virtually synonymous with the series. *Pete Biro photo*

John and Jim Show: Can-Am fans are still talking about Riverside 1966, when Surtees (No. 7 Lola T70) and Hall (No. 66 Chaparral 2E) swapped the lead six times. McLaren's Chris Amon (No. 5 M1B) could only watch, but he had the best seat in the house. *Pete Biro*

Laying the groundwork: Bruce McLaren didn't win any Can-Ams in 1966, though he did start from pole here at Riverside, where his M1B featured experimental fuel injection and driver-operated flipper rear spoiler. *Bob Tronolone*

over backward. Can-Am designers and drivers would learn to manage this danger, but never to eliminate it.

Aerodynamics took on even more significance in the second-ever Can-Am, held at New York's Bridgehampton. That's where Jim Hall stunned the automotive world with his pair of Chaparral 2E-Chevies. His innovative car mounted a wing high atop the rear suspension, directing downforce directly to the rear wheels. That improved traction for better cornering speed and acceleration out of the turn. Once on the straight, the driver's left foot pushed a pedal that tipped the wing level, thus reducing drag.

Hall proved his concept through performance, qualifying on pole. However, both new 2Es had trouble with their wing mechanisms in practice, so only one started the race. Chaparral's Phil Hill—another F1 World Champion—challenged Dan Gurney (Lola-Ford) for the lead until the new aero system acted up again.

Gurney had another challenge just before the end, when Chris Amon nearly caught him. Gurney's

Opposite, top Experience counts: John Surtees, F1 World Champion with Ferrari in 1964, drove his Lola T70 to three first places in 1966 and became the first Can-Am champion. *Pete Biro*

Opposite, bottom Conceptual battle: Jim Hall's fabulous Chaparral 2E (No. 66) showed what the Can-Am car could be, but Bruce McLaren's more conventional, pragmatic M1B (No. 4 McLaren) would point the way to the future. *Pete Biro*

Christopher Racer: That's what his admiring McLaren team called Amon. The young New Zealander had the same fire in his foot as in his eyes. *Dale von Trebra*

Cooper-Ford. One of the earliest sports racing car chassis to get the American hot rod treatment was England's Cooper Monaco. By 1966, the package was no longer competitive, but it still looked fierce, and Nick Adams (shown during an earlier race that summer) did put his on the very first Can-Am grid at St. Jovite. *Dale von Trebra*

Lola T70 just held off Amon's McLaren M1B by 1/5 second. Again, this was a record-setting event in terms of speeds and crowds. It also would remain Ford Motor Company's single Can-Am success.

Mosport Park in Ontario held the next race, the third in as many weekends. Perhaps the strain on people and machinery contributed to what happened at the start: several cars piled up in the first turn. Surtees and Follmer left the scene by ambulance, though neither was seriously hurt.

After a restart, there was racing between Gurney, McLaren, Amon, and newcomer Denis Hulme (Lola-Chevy), but all ran into trouble. So did the Chaparrals of Hall, fastest qualifier again, and Hill. Thus the winner was a surprised Mark Donohue (Lola-Chevy) driving for Roger Penske—remember those names.

Now the Can-Am headed west to Laguna Seca near Monterey in California. Once again Jim Hall took the pole, and this time Phil Hill backed him up for second grid spot, confirming that the innovative Chaparral 2E with its flipper-wing was the new Can-Am's fastest car. For once it stayed fastest, Hill leading bossman Hall to a one-two triumph. Bruce McLaren, who fought the Road Runners hard until his engine acted up, kept it from looking easy, and Parnelli Jones (Lola-Chevy) fought John Surtees off the road in his anxiety to get at the Chaparrals.

Opposite Challman Cherokee Mark 1. The early Can-Am was a hothouse of enthusiastic exploration into novel, unrestricted technologies—engines, transmissions, tires, suspensions, aerodynamics, and materials. Nobody knew the answers; anybody might discover them. California specials builder Bob Challman sportingly decided to offer some developmental help to Lotus creator Colin Chapman, whose first big sports racer, the Lotus 30, wasn't very good, and whose second, the Type 40, was dubbed "The 30 with 10 more mistakes." At Laguna Seca 1966, Challman made the final heat grid via the "consolation" race but retired early. Just behind in the Ferrari Dino coupe at the hairpin is Pedro Rodriguez, who also dropped out. *Bob Tronolone*

Genie Mark 10. Joe Huffaker's roots were in drag racing, but as early as 1954 he built a road racing special to use up parts from a wrecked Austin Healey. Other one-off and limited-production racers followed, the marque name Genie was adopted, and in 1963 came the Super Genie. This was Huffaker's Mark 8, a two-seater designed for small V-8s. To take the torque he crafted his own transaxle, a specially cast magnesium case with Chevrolet gears and a quick-change tail section. Late in 1964 the Mark 10 appeared. This one's space frame was stressed from the outset for the relatively heavy, torquey Chevrolet, the Huffaker transmission was beefed up, hub carriers and brakes were enlarged, and the body was altered to cover wider wheels and tires. Some Mark 8 Genies were updated to Mark 10 specs, of course, but one Mark 10 went the other way. A lightened and downsized car, nicknamed *Vinegaroon* after a scorpion, found victory in the opening USRRC of 1966 at Las Vegas. Charlie Parsons also started that season with a Genie, a Chevy-powered, updated Mark 8. That car is shown in our photo (No. 10), ahead of Lew Florence in a Lotus 19-Ford. Parsons didn't win with it, and midseason switched to a McLaren. Other drivers campaigned Genies in the Can-Am as late as 1968. *Autosport*

The forceful Indianapolis 500 champion actually was up front by the end, but this race had an unusual two-heat format. Having already won the first heat, Hill was safe for the overall victory. Unfortunately, Chaparral's first Johnson Wax trophy would be its last.

Round five was in the Southern California desert at Riverside, notable for a very long straightaway. Here the relatively low-powered Chaparrals (their aluminum Chevrolet engines couldn't be bored out as big as the iron ones) lost the qualifying battle to Bruce McLaren, who took his first pole, and Surtees. McLaren held his starting advantage for the first few laps of the race, but then his engine let him down. That cleared the way for an epic battle between John Surtees and Jim Hall. Pass-and-pass-again; the red Lola T70 and white Chaparral 2E swapped the lead six times that torrid afternoon. The heat of the day finally boiled the Chaparral's fuel, so Hall had to watch Surtees drive away to his second Can-Am win.

In Las Vegas for the sixth and last race, seven drivers still had a chance to be champion. Fearless John Surtees settled it at the first corner of the first lap, shouldering up from fourth grid place into the lead. And there he stayed for the rest of the 210-mile race, clear of the problems that dogged everyone else. His third victory in six starts made Surtees the inaugural Can-Am drivers champion. Coming second on points was Mark Donohue, just ahead of Bruce McLaren.

Word spread quickly, especially in Europe, about how much money they'd won. According to England's *Autosport* magazine, Surtees' total take was "a fantastic $70,000— it was better than winning all of the Formula 1 World Championship races of 1966!" Even Bruce McLaren, though

Hamill SR3. After building an Indy car in 1964, Ed Hamill of Rolling Meadows, Illinois, followed with an SR2 sports car and then a pair of these SR3s in 1965. The one he drove himself (shown ahead of Chris Amon's McLaren M1B at Laguna Seca 1966) had a square-section steel space frame with stiffening panels of aluminum riveted and bonded to it. The other chassis, raced that year by Roy Kumnick, had round-section tubes, but was otherwise similar. After using Ford and Oldsmobile engines initially, Hamill had turned to a Traco-tuned 333 Chevy by this stage. Hamill used McKee transaxles and Ford Mustang brakes. He retired from driving at the end of 1966, and left the sport without finishing a planned SR4. (This and much other helpful information courtesy of the late Doug Waters.) *Bob Tronolone*

Wolverine. Jerry Hansen took this Chevy-powered car to 20th place at St. Jovite. In common with several other one-offs of the era, it was an interesting—and stylish—project, but out of its depth in the rapidly evolving Can-Am. *Lionel Birnbom*

deeply chagrined by his failure to win a single race, admitted that six Can-Ams had brought in more than his three entire F1 seasons to date. Four winning drivers in six events was a good number, and at least three of the six races had been hotly competitive. There had been accidents, but no serious injuries. As for stars, in addition to those in at the beginning, Mario Andretti, A. J. Foyt, Graham Hill, Peter Revson, and Jackie Stewart joined up at various times.

The variety of machinery was fascinating, too. Front-runners Chaparral, Lola, and McLaren were regular entrants that were joined by Brabham, Burnett, Chinook, Cooper, Ferrari, Ford, Genie, Hamill, Lamborghini, Lotus, McKee, Merlyn, Mirage, Porsche, Stanton, Webster, and Wolverine.

Though the Can-Am was a driver's championship, with no formal honor for manufacturers, Lola could justifiably tout its five wins out of six. Chaparral had only one, but in five appearances it took four poles as well as a fastest race lap and scored the only team one-two victory. As for engine makers, no doubt Chevrolet—despite publicly denying any involvement in racing at the time—was proud of its five wins to Ford's one.

By all apparent measures, the bold new Big Banger series was a grand success.

Stanton. This razor-bodied special, which Gene Stanton drove to 18th place in his sole Can-Am appearance, at Bridgehampton 1966, remained the only front-engined car ever to compete in the series. *Pete Lyons*

Mirage. Like most race cars of the era, the Nethercutt Mirage was meant to look at least as good to the eye as to the air. Former Chevrolet stylist and Shelby Cobra Daytona Coupe designer Peter Brock lofted the lissome lines; aerospace engineer Ted Depew drew the small, lightweight chassis, and speced the small, light Olds engine. Grand Prix driver Richie Ginther didn't make the grid here at Riverside, but Scooter Patrick did start the 1966 season finale at Las Vegas. *Bob Tronolone*

PAM. Corvette racing legend Dick Guldstrand still remembers the PAM vividly. "Ah, that was a pretty little car. I raced it first at Laguna Seca, then I flipped it at Riverside. It was aerodynamically terrible, and we didn't know it. I hit those sharks teeth at Turn 2, and it caught wind. I thought, Oh, gee, this might be serious. It was, but I wasn't as upset as the guys who got me out. I had to calm the doctor." Styled by Alexander "Skeets" Kerr, formerly of Shelby American, this special was constructed by German-born Hans Adam to the commission of John "Bat" Masterson. Adam used a few parts from an ex-Jim Clark Lotus 30, which Masterson had crashed. Adam replaced the original monocoque with a steel tube frame and used Corvette components in the suspension. The ill-fated PAM allegedly weighed only 1,020 pounds dry. It was powered by a Shelby-tuned Ford 289. *Bob Tronolone*

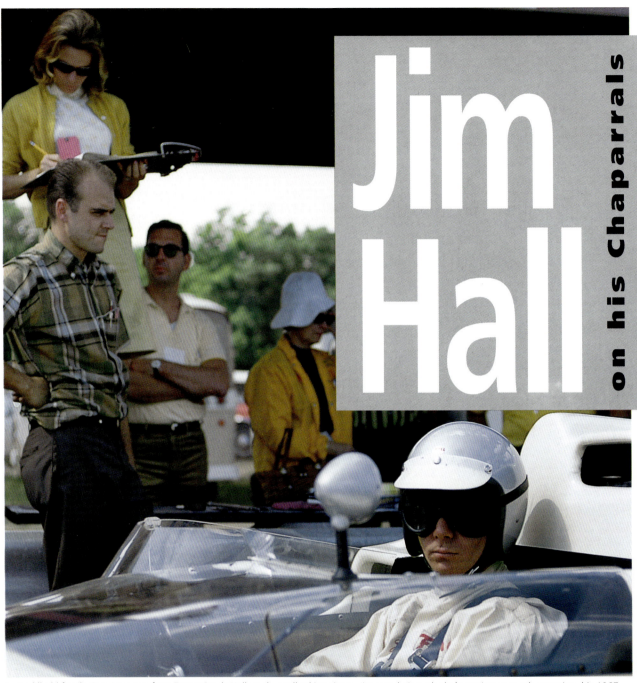

Just a li'l old family Can-Am team from Texas: Sandy Hall on the wall taking times, Jim wondering why he's getting so much attention, his 1967 Chaparral 2G gathering itself to run Road America. Yes, those were pretty casual days everywhere in the sport, but there never would be any pretentiousness at all in one of the remarkable racing organizations of all time. *Pete Lyons*

Jim Hall on his Chaparrals

NO NOVELIST WOULD DARE invent Chaparral Cars. Imagine it: a small, secret race car factory complete with test track hidden away on the plains of West Texas. Though a strictly private operation, it enjoys a clandestine link to the world's largest automaker. Magically, from this implausible place appear machines so advanced that they change the very shape of world motorsport—not to mention the text of international rules books.

Impossible . . . but it happened. Cal Tech graduate engineer Jim Hall and his friend Hap Sharp, successful oilmen and fine sports car racers both, really did create homebuilt specials that beat the world's best marques. Hall drove one to the 1964 United States Road Racing Championship, and in 1965 he and Sharp shared Chaparral's victory in the Sebring 12-Hour Grand Prix of Endurance. Named after the Road Runner bird of the American Southwest, their cars also won long-distance events in Europe.

The white wonders from Texas opened eyes by their technical innovation as well as their speed. Composite chassis structures, all the rage today, were introduced to racing in 1963 by the Chaparral 2A's fiberglass monocoque. Chaparrals also were known for aerodynamic surprises. Understandably, motorsports-minded engineers at Chevrolet R&D were fascinated by these ingenious specials powered by hot-rodded Chevy engines. Also understandably, they soon began helping out—in defiance of a corporate ban on racing involvement. From GM's back door in Michigan flowed a wealth of experimental aluminum engines, torque converter transmissions, and other trick hardware that Hall and his boys in Midland obligingly race-tested for their friends up North.

If Chaparrals had one signature feature, it was the tall, suspension-mounted, driver-adjustable "flipper" wing. Hall and four GM engineers patented the idea, which was used on the 2E and 2G Can-Am roadsters of 1966-1968 as well as 1967's 2F endurance racing coupe.

Ingenious design features earned Chaparral Cars a unique reputation, but too often gave teething troubles during races. This constructor, seemingly born to the wide-open Can-Am series, won just a single race,

The racing partnership of James "Hap" Sharp (left) and Jim Hall blossomed into the creation of Chaparral Cars. Hall feels that his late friend deserves wider recognition for his contribution to their overall success as well as for his driving ability. *Pete Biro*

Laguna Seca 1966. Founding partner Hap Sharp eventually retired, and Jim Hall suffered a bad accident in 1968 at Las Vegas. More fun was taken out of the game for him when sanctioning bodies outlawed such Chaparral innovations as the suspension-mounted wing. After the 1970 ban of his (and Chevrolet's) Model 2J Ground Effect Vehicle, a.k.a. "The Sucker," Hall left this no-longer unlimited form of racing which he'd done so much to establish. In later programs with other kinds of cars, his teams won many more races, including two Indianapolis 500s, but it is with his early sports cars that Jim Hall will always be most closely identified. His comments about them were drawn from several interviews for *Autosport, AutoWeek,* and *Vintage Motorsport* magazines.

I had a lot of fun in the 1960s, because we were pretty much on the forward edge of chassis development of race cars. To be doing things that were a little bit original, to not just take somebody

37

Ironically, these cars named after the Road Runner—a bird that seldom flies—became world leaders in aerodynamic research. The Chaparral 2 of 1963–1965 (pictured in 1965 at Watkins Glen) predated the Can-Am series, but it taught Jim Hall and his team the importance of downforce. *Pete Lyons*

else's idea and work on it but to think of a better way to do it, I really did enjoy that. . . . I'm just a kid who never grew up!

One of the fun parts, of course, was that I got to do a lot of the test driving. I bet I drove 100 days a year. That gave me an advantage compared to other guys at the time, I think. And when the car wouldn't do something that I wanted it to do, we tried to think of a way to do it. To go out there and compensate for the car, just use your physical skills to get the best you can out of a car that's not quite right, I'm not as an engineer satisfied with that. My mind is always saying, "What should I be doing to get rid of this problem in the car?"

We worked very, very hard on trying to make the cars really comfortable to drive. I've always

Chaparral's Jim Hall, driver, engineer, and visionary, co-created the wonderful winged Road Runners from Texas that forever stand tall as the very definition of "Unlimited Can-Am car." Here he flies his Chaparral 2G around Laguna Seca early in 1968. *Pete Biro*

felt if the physical effort was low, and if you could more play it like a musical instrument than horse it around like a cowboy, and you could stay cool, you'd be in a lot better shape—especially in the last 10 laps.

So the seats were molded to fit the individual, and we had pads that came up and held you under your arms very securely so that you didn't rattle around in there. It was almost like an extension of you. I was always meticulous about throttle position. See, with two pedals [thanks to the torque converter transmission, there was no clutch], you don't have to move your feet around very much. I had heel rests on the floor so that I could brace my feet, and I could *squeeze* the throttle rather than have to punch at it. My hands fell naturally on the steering wheel, because I put it right where I wanted it.

And then we reduced all the forces, the brake forces and the accelerator pedal force and the steering force, to where it was not physically hard to drive. I always felt that would allow you to drive the car more precisely and

On its debut at Bridgehampton 1966 (where Phil Hill leads the McLarens of Chris Amon and Bruce McLaren), the winged Chaparral 2E was a startling sight to eyes that were still adjusting to midengined cars. It looks nearly as strange today, thanks to rules imposed to restrict many Chaparral innovations. *Pete Lyons*

Creative right to its core, Chaparral brought the aerospace concept of composite chassis into racing in 1963—two decades before Formula One came around to the idea. (By the time of the Can-Am series, Chaparral had gone back to aluminum monocoques, only using a "plastic chassis" once more, in 1969.) *Autosport*

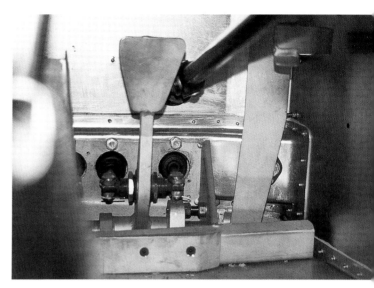

Chaparrals were painstakingly developed for driver-friendliness. This is the cockpit of a restored 2E, photographed recently at Chaparral Cars—a feat difficult in 1966! Thanks to Chevrolet's torque converter, there is no clutch pedal. In its place is one that feathers the rear wing for low drag on straights. When this is released, the wing automatically flips to its high-drag, high-stability position. The driver brakes with the left foot, keeping the right on the gas pedal. Though often called an "automatic," the transmission is shifted only with a manual gear shift lever. First gear is engaged before the engine is started, then the car is held stationary with the brake. Once under way, shifts up or down are made by moving the lever and simultaneously lifting or blipping the throttle. In that respect it's similar to the way typical Hewlands and other manual racing boxes can be driven, although Chaparrals never had more than three forward gears. *Pete Lyons*

faster, rather than having to be forcing it with your muscles.

So by the time we built the Es [1966 Model 2E], we had pretty well zeroed-in on that. . . . I thought they were very, very easy and precise to drive. Phil Hill was surprised at how nice they were to drive, and he'd driven a lot of cars. The forces were pretty high on you, because the cars cornered at high G-loads, and they'd stop fast, and they were light and accelerated good. But the seats, the belts, the way you sat in the car, allowed you to take those forces really well.

The cars themselves were a pretty good package in 1966. They handled good, they stopped good, they did a lot of things right. We had some problems, but I think I was really in the hunt for the Can-Am championship right up to Riverside. Then Surtees beat me. I was so much quicker than he was . . . until my fuel started vaporizing.

What was Hap Sharp's role?

He was a big contributor to the whole thing. Hap was a genuine partner. He had his drilling business to run, but he was there [at Chaparral Cars] most days, and a lot of the ideas came from him, from his interest. He had a lot of good ideas—lot of bad ideas, too! We were really interested in what we were doing. We thought and slept race car driving, and when we went out to dinner we talked about it. When we got drunk, we got drunk thinking about race cars, and if we remembered anything in the morning, we wrote it down and went on.

One time in 1964 I went to a race in the Southeast somewhere, before we had but one of those cars [early 2A]. And Hap, for some reason he made a deal to drive an Elva-Porsche down there. He'd been driving our cars, and we'd already discovered that we had to have downforce on the back of them. He came in and said, "Geesh, this thing oversteers like hell at fast corners. What about putting a piece of metal up on the back and making a little spoiler?" And I said, "Ooh hell, don't do that. You know, if you do that and go faster, everybody's going to do it." So he didn't. He was a good team player.

I never thought Hap got the recognition he deserved as a driver. He was damn quick, he was as competitive as could be. I can remember times when I couldn't beat him. I thought to myself, "Dammit, if he weighs 50 pounds more than I do, why am I not beating him?" So he was doing something better than I was doing. I've driven against a lot of people who were highly rated, and I know what they can do in a lot of areas. I rate Hap pretty darn good as a driver.

How did the hookup with
Chevrolet come about?

Through Bill Mitchell, the styling head of GM—he was interested in racing, and he always took some of his show cars up to Elkhart Lake. When we had the front-engined Chaparral there in 1962, Bill and I got acquainted, and he said, "Why don't you come over and see all my new toys at Styling some day?" Hap and I thought, well, that's a good connection. Let's do it.

We were building the Chaparral 2 [later known as the 2A] at that time. Bill had designed something called a Corvair Monza [auto show concept car], beautiful little car. Our car ended up looking quite a bit like that.

They didn't actually style your car?

No, I just used the same wind tunnel data. [Corvette stylist] Larry Shinoda was there then, pushing clay [creating body prototypes], and he had done some wind tunnel work [on the Monza show car]. When I was up there one day, he gave me a copy of the study.

Bill Mitchell also introduced me to Frank Winchell, who was in charge of a little Chevrolet division called R&D. They had built a monocoque chassis out of steel for that Monza car. We got to talking, because we built ours out of fiberglass, and he was interested in why. That was the best introduction I had as far as Chevrolet was concerned, because Frank and I hit it off real well.

I got to go to the proving ground some time in the next year to drive the Corvair [production model]. All this rhubarb about the Corvair [handling] was beginning to happen. Frank Winchell really wanted to understand why the race cars could have rear weight distribution and be good cars, and yet everybody was saying this Corvair they built was junk. So I spent a lot of time driving it through esses and around skid pads for him at high load.

So the infamous
Corvair debacle
advanced motor
racing science?

Helped me. Because I got to know some guys that were really interested in vehicle dynamics, just like I was.

Did Chaparral's
aerodynamic
development have
anything to do
with your interest
in aircraft?

I'm sure that had some effect on it. I knew how airplanes worked, and what those forces were, and how you dealt with them.

I'm probably more responsible for down-force on race cars than

Hall said later that turning his original light, sweet-handling 2E into 1967's big block 2G was a mistake. Rivals weren't so sure at the time, judging from the expressions on McLaren's Teddy Mayer (standing in front of car) and Penske's Mark Donohue (near right rear wheel) at Elkhart Lake. *Pete Lyons*

Hall

By 1970, life as a Road Runner was different. After suffering severe leg injuries in a 1968 crash, Jim was no longer driving his own cars. Nor was he having much fun on the technical side, because in a changed Can-Am climate, Chaparral innovation was receiving more protest than praise. The 2J car itself gave constant trouble. Here Hall, former Chevrolet engineer Don Gates, and driver Vic Elford ponder yet another problem at Road Atlanta. *Pete Lyons*

anybody I know of. Because I really did grasp that from the driver seat and from the engineering [side] of it. I think we probably had a little better idea of what the aerodynamics of those cars were in those days and how to deal with it than anybody else.

We got involved in the aerodynamics real early because the first Chaparral, the front engine car that Troutman and Barnes built [1961 Type 1], had a lift problem. You know, we tried venturi ground effects, shapes on the underside of the car to produce a download. We just kept thinking that if we could get the pressure low under the car, that would help. That was in our mind all the time. We were unsuccessful, because we didn't understand it very well.

The first midengine car [1963 2A] had a bad lift problem. The body was based pretty much on that GM wind tunnel study. It was kind of an upside-down wing idea. When we put it on the racetrack, it was awful. The front end lifted so bad that it was virtually undrivable. The front wheels actually came off the ground at 120 miles per hour. It was so bad I had to solve it, and I did [with a "snowplow" front spoiler].

Then I thought that really what I'd like to have is a car that doesn't lift. We clayed up and built a lot of stuff [new body profiles], and tried it out. I got some instrumentation—in fact, the first instrumentation was just a piece of welding rod wrapped around the front suspension and stuck up through a hole in the fender. We'd calibrate it and drive at 100 miles per hour, and see how much lift we had. We made enough modifications on the front of the car to get it where it was zero lift. Then we got the back where it was zero.

Well, what I found out was, that wasn't a good race car. I could run it on the skid pad, and it was balanced well at 40 miles per hour. But I'd take it out to the high-speed turns, and it would oversteer. So I had to put some lift back into the front in order to balance it out at high speed.

I got to thinking about it some more, and I said to myself, "Gee, if we've got all this force, why not use it to some advantage? If I could just push down on the back, that must be better." So that's where the first little duck-tail came from, on our car, anyway. We just put a piece of sheet metal up on the back.

Were you aware of the rear spoiler that Richie Ginther invented for Ferrari in 1961?

I realized that they had that little duck-tail on the back, but I didn't know what it was. That hadn't all gone together in my mind. But as soon as we put any download on the back of our car, the lap times just dropped dramatically. We started putting more and more download on the cars, and they just got faster and faster and faster. That was the lights-on, I think, when we said "Push down on it." From there on it was development, just a logical, natural progression.

Originally built by Chevrolet R&D as a test bed, not a race car, the Chaparral 2J Ground Effect Vehicle was heavy and complex. But it could get around a track quickly when everything was working properly. A two-cylinder auxiliary motor located above the rear axle line powered a pair of belt-driven, ducted fans on the stern to extract air from the car's interior. A system of Lexan plastic skirts, which were linked through cables to the suspension to maintain a constant height, preserved a minimum air gap around the bottom of the car. In principle, the car acted like a suction cup to press its tires onto the road, independently of its forward speed. *Pete Lyons*

Eventually we got them to where they had so much drag that, even though we could lap faster than the other cars, we couldn't beat them on the racetrack, because we couldn't pass them. We were so slow down the straightaways that once they blew you off, you couldn't catch them on braking, and they could block you in the turns. You might be able to lap faster, but you couldn't work your way through traffic.

So that's when the little flip-flop flap happened [the body-mounted, driver-operated flipper on the 2C of 1965]. That fixed that, so that we could run just about as fast down the straightaway, and we still had the cornering. Of course once we had the flap moveable, we made it so big that we bottomed out on the suspension. We kept having to go to higher rear spring rates and we didn't like it, because that meant we had to go to higher front spring rates to make the thing handle on the slow turns. We didn't have the tires, then, to make the car work over the bumps with those high spring rates. It was pretty much undrivable again.

So I think the thought mechanism was, "Get rid of those high spring rates . . . hook the wing to the hub." That development of the car as a handling package was really nice. You could take it to any racetrack in the world and set it up so it was very, very drivable. Because you didn't have real high-rate springs, and you could control the car over the bumps with the shocks and the springs. Yet you had a lot of download, which was adjustable front to back. So by just changing the bars and the wing settings, in a matter of a couple of hours you had a setup that was really nice. The cars were faster again, better again. I was disappointed when that all got thrown by the wayside.

What about the 2J Ground Effects Vehicle, the so-called Sucker?

Well, the sucker car really came about as a result of the FIA ban on wings [implemented in 1969]. I used to go back up to R&D at Chevrolet and talk about race results with the engineers there. That was one of the things that they got out of the relationship, first-hand information. They were gaining knowledge.

It was in one of those round table discussions that somebody said, "You know, Hovercraft, if you sucked instead of blew, that'd create a hell of a lot of downforce." It wasn't my idea, but I had seen it

45

before. As a matter of fact, some kid had sent me a sketch of one before that time. But it wasn't me in that meeting that said, "Gee, we ought to build something like that." It was somebody else. They decided that it was a worthwhile investment on their part to build a test car to do that.

Were you initially skeptical of the ground effects car?

No, I just didn't have time to mess with it. We were building the 2H at that time [1968-69], and it turned into a handful. So the guys at Chevy went ahead and built the J-car [1970 2J]—which it wasn't called then, it was just another GM test car originally.

When my H-car was so unsuccessful, we really had egg on our face. I got some vibes from Chevrolet, well why don't you take the vacuum car and run it? But that's scary, when you stop and think about how complicated it is. It's got a system of skirts on it that are all articulated, and it takes guys looking after that. And it's got an auxiliary engine that runs the fans. Plus, it's a race car in addition to that. So compared with the cars we were running, it took about twice the number of people just to go out and test it. If you took it to a racetrack it would be a real scene.

But they said, "You know, this is really an original idea, and somebody's gonna do it if we don't do it." Eventually I said, "Ship it down here and we'll see what we can do with it." They did and we tested it a lot and tried to make it into something. We committed to go the 1970 season with it eventually. It really wasn't ready to go racing. It was still a test car. We needed another year. There were too many problems.

There was a lot of controversy, too, about new SCCA rules that required " coachwork" to be fixed in place. But didn't somebody from the club pass the car before it appeared?

Yeah, Jim Kaser, the chairman, and the technical guy, John Timanus. They came and looked at it. "Well, we don't see any reason it isn't legal." I pressed on.

Then why the about-face at the end of the year?

You know, I wasn't involved in that discussion. They had a Can-Am owners meeting of some kind that I didn't even know about, which was kind of odd. That happened in California after the Riverside race, apparently. A bunch of the other guys, amongst them I think some of the manufacturers, said, "It's going to ruin the series." That's like they do, you know. I don't know exactly what was said, but from there on it progressed to being illegal. I'm not sure exactly how that went on.

Would you have continued for 1971 had the car not been banned?

I think so. It showed enough promise during 1970. We took it to Watkins Glen; we were third on the grid with Jackie Stewart behind Denny and Bruce. It was fun to have him introduce it. I really enjoyed him.

For a race driver in those days, he was expensive for me, so we got Vic Elford to drive it. His first race, Road Atlanta, he was on the pole, blew them off by a second. Our last race, Riverside, he was over two seconds faster. So the progression that we made with it was pretty damn good for the amount of time involved. It never did run very long in a race. I think Atlanta was the only race it finished in the whole series. But we would have figured a way to go on with it, because it had a hell of a lot of potential. We were just kind of scratching the surface, really.

McLaren had that long string of success . . .

Yeah. Boy, that was fantastic.

Their approach was very different from yours, much more conservative. Did you ever have the feeling that maybe you were out-tricking yourself? That maybe you should have stepped back and built a more conventional car?

I think to win races you do it with the more conventional car. I agree with that. I guess if I had said to myself, "The most important thing is for us to win races. . . ."

Hap had already concluded that. His statement was, "You win races in obsolete race cars." That's kind of a funny statement, but the way he meant it was, last year's race car is more proven and fast enough. The car that was a little older and more reliable, he was perfectly happy to drive.

I took the position that, well, I'll take the new stuff and I'll see what I can do with it. So it made a good team, because he never pressed me and said, "Your car might be faster than mine, why don't I take it?" I was working on the car to try to make it faster, that was kind of my part of the job. I was pushing ahead. I guess that was just as important to me as winning races.

Must have been, or I wouldn't have done it that way.

Do you see any possibility of reviving the original Can-Am idea of unlimited technology?

There's no way to go back, is there? Once it's done, it's done, and everybody goes forward from there. That's all in the past.

So that was kind of a Golden Age?

It was fun to do as individuals doing it when it could be done that way. Once it gets to where it takes five engineers, draftsmen and all that staff just to go out there and run, well . . .

One of the beauties of being a race car builder in the time that I did it was the fact that it could be a one-man show. I could have ideas and produce them and try them, and find out whether they were any good or not. I got to actually feel the car was better, and it went faster. That's one of the nice things about racing, that you get instant feedback.

We had a lot of people here, but it was really fun to feel responsible for a lot of that, that I was shaping it and pushing it along and making it happen. Probably the most fun time of my life.

Accustomed to working up their secrets in the solitude of West Texas, Chaparral people were very security-minded at the track. Prepping the 2J the night before Riverside 1970, Troy Rogers did not welcome a furtive visitor. (Actually, Troy is a really friendly guy, and a master craftsman who has proudly restored every surviving Chaparral to running condition.) *Pete Lyons*

Phil Hill, America's first World Driving Champion and winner of Chaparral's one Can-Am victory. Here at Bridgehampton 1966, he gets comfortable in the 2E he'll be racing for the first time. *Pete Lyons*

Phil Hill

FOR THOSE OF US WHO appreciate racing machines as tangible expressions of advanced human thought, the Chaparral era was vividly exciting. It was the 1960s, that period of such tumultuous change in American society at large, and the tall white Road Runners from west Texas were the boldest revolutions in motorsports. Most race cars of the time were primarily the products of experience, intuition, and faith. The Chaparrals, built by partners Jim Hall and Hap Sharp in their obscure, shed-like skunkworks on the lonely plains south of Midland, really did spring from science. And, to the eyes of tradition, they did look strange.

The original, no-holds-barred Can-Am seemed made for Chaparrals, and certainly the first Chaparral made for the Can-Am took full advantage of the freedom. The model 2E of 1966 simply sparkled with science. Built as compactly and as light in weight as possible, it had a small block Chevrolet engine specially cast in aluminum, a Chevrolet-built transmission featuring a torque converter instead of a clutch, and radiators in the body sides rather than the nose. But what really startled the eyes of 1966 was the 2E's variable aerodynamic downforce system.

Eyes first fell on a large, articulated airfoil (Jim Hall called it a "flipper") standing high above the tail on struts mounted, not to the body or chassis, but directly to the rear wheel hub carriers. Closer examination revealed another aerodynamic device sunk into the otherwise empty "radiator duct" in the nose of the car. Good spies soon learned that both flippers were controlled by the driver's left foot on a pedal that occupied the place of a conventional car's clutch pedal.

"Weird," said many people. "Outlandish" or "crazy," said others. "Strange," thought Phil Hill. Until he drove it. Then he found Chaparral's startling science made the 2E generally the fastest car of that first Can-Am season. Unfortunately, it was far from the most reliable, suffering wing-mount and wing-actuation failures in particular. But the 1961 World Driving Champion did lead his boss to a fine one-two finish—Chaparral's only Can-Am victory—at Laguna Seca 1966.

When I first got to Chaparral Cars, it seemed strange to see this funny little place down in the middle of nowhere. The wind seemed to be blowing all the time. It was strange that so many great cars came from this seemingly primitive environment.

Which it wasn't. Not at all. Jim Hall was such a tremendous pioneer; he was really doing it scientifically. It was the first time that you could ever see your way to having a car that was all good. Earlier, we had to live with the good and the bad.

Of course, they did their best to keep their drivers from knowing about the relationship between Chevrolet and them. Maybe they thought that we couldn't keep our mouths shut. You weren't made to feel like an outsider, really, but the degree of insideness that you could have felt was restricted. So I can't really tell you how much of Chaparral was just local brilliance, which they wanted us to think. I know that Jim is a sharp guy, no question about it, but they had a lot of interesting people from up North.

I didn't have a great experience the first time I drove the 2E, at Bridgehampton. The wings failed on both cars, and I was driving both times. The first time, a bolt broke and rubbed on a tire, and it popped, and I went up the embankment. Jim said, "Well, take my car." I said, "Well . . . OK." First time I'd driven the darned thing. The second time it happened I was ready for it, and I could see it in my shadow. I was going down a straight with the sun behind me, and I could see the shadow of the wing on the

The space age Chaparral of 1966 was fast, but not yet fully developed. Jim Hall actually made fastest qualifying speed at Bridgehampton, but after both 2Es had wing mount trouble in practice, he handed his car to Phil Hill for the race. Before more trouble cropped up, Hill was ahead of the McLarens. Here Bruce McLaren and Chris Amon trail, as the trio swoops through the Long Island sand dunes past Gene Stanton's front-engined homebuilt. *Pete Lyons*

Not just a new look in race cars, the 2E was the first to treat the atmosphere as a friend. With the wing at its optimum angle of attack, the downforce went straight to the rear tires for better braking, cornering, and acceleration without need of stiffer springs. When the driver leveled the "flipper," its drag disappeared. *Pete Lyons*

road ahead, and all of a sudden the darned struts flopped over.

When that car was right, it was quick. With the wing [in high-downforce position] you could out-brake everybody, you could out-corner everybody, you could drive under them, you could do everything. It really did feel like it had freak roadholding.

On fast parts of the circuit, you pushed the pedal. That trimmed the wing out and did some things up front that made the car every bit as nicely balanced, except much more slippery. That's how you thought of [operating the wing]. You didn't think of it for extra downforce, you thought of it as extra speed.

The wing pedal had an over-center feel to it, so you didn't have to waste any energy in holding it down there. It sort of held itself. But the faster you went the harder it was to get it into that position, so you had to remember to get it into the low-drag mode before you were going too fast. Later on, he managed to rig up some little trim-tab gadgetry to let us have our cake and eat it too.

With the torque converter transmission, you braked with your left foot, and it was just so nice to keep your right foot on the go pedal. Places where you had these short little squirts, it paid. You were able to make the switch between on and off a tiny bit quicker than the next guy.

It did take a particular technique to shift. You shifted as if you had no clutch, just back off and push it out of gear and time it into the next one as if you were using a clutch, except there wasn't any. Jim used to complain continually about how he was the only one whose transmission looked nice when they would take it apart. I think I was next. But some of the guys could really make a mess of them.

It's just really unfortunate that the Chaparrals had to be cursed with bad luck. Those cars were so great.

The Can-Am, gosh, I just thought that its breadth and concept, that it sort of had an open formula to it, made it just as exciting as anything. It appealed to the spectator in a particularly wonderful way. It was just wonderful that it did exist in those years.

After winning one-two at Laguna Seca, Chaparral had a disastrous 1966 season finale at Las Vegas, with more airfoil system trouble. Hall retired, but Hill continued after his wing was replaced by the spacer bar normally installed during transport. Deprived of rear downforce, the 2E was very hard to handle, and there was an incident with another car. *Pete Biro*

John Surtees

Fearless John Surtees was incredibly fast on two and four wheels. He added Formula 1 and Can Am titles to his list of accomplishments, which included several motorcycle world championships. Here in the pit lane at Elkhart Lake, 1967, Surtees was about to defend his Can-Am championship. Unfortunately, the new Lola wasn't up to the job. *Pete Lyons*

FEARLESS JOHN SURTEES; if you knew nothing else about him, his seven world championships on Grand Prix motorcycles plus his 1964 F1 driving title with Ferrari would give you some idea of his ability, ambition and steely resolve. Having race-prepared his own bikes as a youngster, he always remained deeply involved on the mechanical side, and found Big Banger sports cars irresistible. Surtees worked with Lola to develop the beautiful and successful T70, scoring its first race wins in 1965. Despite suffering severe injuries later that year when a T70 broke under him, in 1966 he was back to lead the Lola factory team in the inaugural Can-Am series—and to win the championship.

John generously sat for my tape recorder twice, first at his Team Surtees office in England in 1994, and again at Motegi, Japan, in 1998. The following quotations combine those interviews.

The team was a trailer, one Chevy van, and one mechanic, Malcolm Malone, who was also the van driver. One car, two engines. Little team. What we managed on was enthusiastic helpers who came along and gave Malcolm a helping hand.

Our first race was St. Jovite, and we had a good dice with Bruce McLaren. That was a good win, because there's a sheer driver's circuit. I always remember with affection that turn after the pits, where it went down, up and then down again. The car could come right off the road there. It was to start with a little bit frightening, but it's the quick stuff where you have to pick up time, and when you get those things right, they're the ones that give you satisfaction.

The first Can-Am ever was one of the best ever. At St. Jovite 1966, Surtees (No. 3 Lola T70) had a crowd-thrilling pass and pass again dice with Bruce McLaren (M1B) that went on for 2 hours and 6 minutes. During the tight six-race season, Surtees won three rounds and the inaugural series title. *Lionel Birnbom/Road & Track*

Of course, we had the worries about how you went over that hump in the so-called straight, because Hugh Dibley and Paul Hawkins turned their cars over backwards. I didn't have that problem. I think because of my motorcycling career, the fact that you've got a number of places, such as the Isle of Man, where you flew up the air. I probably got the approach to it better. You were quicker by actually coming off the gas and getting the nose down for a moment. With the Can-Am car, the last thing you wanted to do when you came to that peak was to be with your foot in it.

And also, of course, the aerodynamic balance of your car is important. Lots of people put very big dams up the back on those sorts of circuits, which may make the thing feel that much better or induce more understeer. In the Lola, particularly, that was the case. But I tried to refrain from that, because one, it knocked off the speed, and two, you could have this problem on the hump.

The Lola T70 at that stage was a good driver's car, which you could drive very hard, and it was fun to drive. I've always tried to develop a car to where it gives a reasonably consistent message. When it reaches its optimum performance, when you've got it right up there to the very edge, you'll often get it to become just a little nervous. A car that is all the time forgiving is not necessarily a quick car. But with the Can-Am, to a large extent you were dealing with a relatively large lump of a motor car, and you had to have a car which was pretty predictable, that didn't have any really nasty vices. Because, of course, it was a car that was built to be sold—and it was the most popular production car of its time.

This is the way the T70 was tested and developed, always working totally in conjunction with Eric Broadley [Lola's Technical Director], to a point where the car could be driven hard and would give you a good message, without having to put more aerodynamics on it to push it down. It was basically quite an efficient car, which had that ability to mate to the driver.

It was a little harder on brakes and things, because it weighed more than the McLaren. McLaren had settled for a light, very maneuverable car, which certainly by itself was capable of doing as quick a time as anything. But what aided me largely, and it happened in more than one event, neither Bruce McLaren nor Chris Amon were real scratchers. They were quick, but they would not do anything desperate—not like a Jack Brabham who, if you gave an inch to, would scratch the corner away from you and arrive in a big heap with everything locked up. Chris and Bruce were predictable drivers. They wouldn't normally do anything particularly unusual; they'd be quite conventional.

So you could work out what you could do and what you couldn't do, and knowing the characteristics of your own car, you'd know where you could pick them up. Well, Bruce was very capable and the McLaren was very nimble, but with its smaller engine it relied on maximum cornering speed to get its speed down the straight. We found if you got in front, then you could control the race from the front. You could actually sort of slow the pace of the race below what you were capable of, and they still couldn't get by you.

Particularly with Can-Am cars, you didn't want to win the race any faster than you could possibly help. Because, you know, they weren't the most reliable.

Winning the first race got you off to a good start, but the next few weekends didn't go so well.

Bridgehampton; each time I went to Bridgehampton it was a bit of a disaster [in 1966 Surtees had gearbox and oil line problems]. Strange, because the circuit actually wasn't a bad circuit. Mosport, we got munched up the back at the start. At Laguna Seca, Parnelli Jones shunted me off. I suppose if you've got somebody behind you and you allow him to do that to you, you're as much a fool as he. The old Indy drivers from that period were a different breed.

Then at Riverside you won one of the best Can-Am duels ever, when you and Jim Hall in the Chaparral 2E swapped the lead seven times before his engine vapor-locked.

It was a big race there. Jim of course was able to feather his wing, and it was the alloy-block engine, very light. That was a good package. The whole thing was so logical in its own way, wasn't it? I'd love to have tried that car.

And Jim in a Chaparral was a good competitor. He was together with his motor car, and he would have a fair old go. It was very much a case of slipstreaming him, and one of the big places to pass was coming into that last turn—a big out-braking job. And that was important, because if you could outbrake him there, it meant that you controlled the line past the start and into the very wiggly bit, where he was able to put on so much downforce. Through the tight stuff, he was quicker.

But the Lola worked well [on the straight], we were running minimum flap and things on it. So the race had that pattern: he'd out-squirt me coming through the hairpin onto the long straight, I'd get right in the slipstream, he'd drag me along, and then I'd have to try to out-brake him again.

Oh, that was a good race.

So was Las Vegas, for you.

Vegas was quite a tough race. Luckily, it was the sort of circuit where you could scratch 'round. Through the back there, it was quite quick.

I don't think we qualified well, and then we took a bit of a challenge for the race and changed some gear to try to improve things. We did, and I made a good start, managed to nip in front at the first corner. Then I was able to control the race.

So we had varying fortunes during the year, but we ended up at Vegas just sort of snaffling it. It was good to compete with our little shoestring team, very satisfactory. We seized the day when it could be seized, and it was more of a level playing field. On the whole, we didn't have much luck again.

To defend your championship in 1967, Lola gave you a revised T70 Mark IIIb roadster. You didn't like it.

I had done hardly any running in the modified cars, because they were late. I was very unhappy with the engine and the handling. A few corners were cut to save weight, and a number of geometry changes were made in the suspension. They didn't work. The car lost the predictability that it originally had.

For the last event of the year, Las Vegas, I thought at least we must try and finish properly, so we dumped the fresh car and went and got our old race car back from [Lola importer] Carl Haas, that was sitting up in his showroom. We actually won, using the old original car and the previous year's engines.

Surtees

In hindsight, I think that the Can-Am program should have been taken a lot more seriously by both myself and Eric Broadley. It was a question of when you had a moment to spare, you took your mind to it. Eric was spreading himself a bit thin, and my prime consideration was Formula One. Whereas for McLaren, I think it's fair to say, the Number One thing at that stage was sports cars. They had quite a good American management in Teddy Mayer. They had lots of American contacts. So they were well positioned, and Bruce and company started a very sensible program and built on it.

For your third Can-Am campaign, 1968, you joined the general move to Chevrolet's big block engine, but tried to go one step better with special cylinder heads. These were commissioned from Britain's famed Weslake Engineering, whose heads were on that year's Le Mans–winning Ford GT40, and who

In 1968 Surtees tried English heads on his American Chevy.

also had built Dan Gurney's V-12 Formula One engines. Unfortunately, Team Surtees' Chevy project became an object lesson in how not to go Can-Am racing. You only made three races of the six, and didn't finish any.

In 1968, Bruce McLaren got the deal for the big Chevrolet engines, so that put us in a position. I took a chance and bought a couple of aluminum blocks, and I hoped that Weslake Engineering would be the answer. My theory was that, if we put a bit more modern technology in the heads based on the experience Weslakes had gained in porting, we should improve the performance. Possibly we would get an edge in compactness as well, without these great big induction trumpets sticking up in front of the wings like normal Chevys have, due to their enormous ports. That would help the aerodynamics. It was a very neat, nice package to put in the car, with the Lucas injection. It looked super.

Unfortunately it was a disaster. Weslakes had internal problems. We received lots of assurances as to what would happen and when it would happen, but unfortunately the end result was that, I think rather like poor Dan Gurney found out, nothing was done on time. No two pieces were the same. We ended up with the first engine being assembled with all different valve timing because of rockers being different on virtually each valve. The pistons that came were not as they were designed. So the engines never got finished in time, never got tested, and never produced the power.

We had a very sick time in 1968.

Surtees' final Can-Am season was spent struggling with Chaparral's radical and recalcitrant 2H. *Pete Lyons*

1967: Kiwi Domination

Bruce and Denny Play America

The new season began at a fresh venue, Wisconsin's Elkhart Lake, and on a novel note: a crushing victory by McLaren. But what earned that result was old-fashioned hard work on a well-seasoned car.

McLaren's was a formula that seems so obvious in hindsight, even deceptively simple. Many rivals saw it at the time. But whatever the reasons, for the next five years nobody but Bruce McLaren Motor Racing would be able to marshal the mix of pragmatically advanced design, thorough preseason testing, engineering and driving talent, and well-managed money that brought success in the Can-Am.

Add motivation. Though he'd been competitive in 1966, the New Zealander hadn't won. He took it as a personal failure, as did his whole team.

By the opening day of 1967, they were more than ready. Bruce put his startlingly caramel-colored McLaren-Chevy M6A on the pole at time over 10 seconds better than the Elkhart track record. Backing him up for the front row, a scant tenth-second slower, was his fellow Kiwi and new team mate, Denny-the-Bear Hulme (Chris Amon had gone to Ferrari, which didn't make it to this first race). Dan Gurney was the best of the rest, nearly two seconds back, in his suddenly old-fashioned–looking Lola T70-Ford.

At flagfall, Denny spurted straight into the lead and cruised on to an untroubled victory by over a minute and a half. Bruce did retire with engine failure, but the sight of him trudging back to the pits couldn't have been very encouraging to other drivers. McLaren had made them all backmarkers, and they knew it.

Stardust Can-Am, Las Vegas 1967: Jim Hall (No. 66 Chaparral 2G) leading Bruce McLaren (No. 4 McLaren M6A) and Parnelli Jones (No. 21 Lola T79) on the pace lap. *Claire Lyons McHenry*

The McLaren team rubbed it in at Bridgehampton. Denny won again, from pole this time, and at a new track record. This time Bruce lasted and took second-place points and prize monies.

Round three at Mosport was a little more dramatic. Though Hulme and McLaren once more dominated the front row, on race morning Bruce's car sprang a fuel leak, and it wasn't fixed until the field was halfway around the first racing lap. Later on, Denny's steering broke and he hit an embankment. So who won? Mr. Hulme, in a comet of smoke, his left front fender smashed and the tire flat. And in second place? Mr. McLaren, of course, after a crowd-stirring charge up through the entire field.

The season's field included good drivers in cars that would have looked fast if only the new

Color me Kiwi: McLaren's eye-popping new livery was just the beginning. At Road America's Round 1, Bruce (seated in the M6A), Tyler Alexander (left), and Colin Beanland are about to lift Can-Am to a new level of competition. *Pete Biro*

Below::
Done deal: By Las Vegas, the McLaren team had wrapped up the series with five straight wins. The only thing left to decide was whether Hulme (No. 5, leading the pace lap at Turn 2) or McLaren himself would take home the trophy. *Claire Lyons McHenry*

American innovation: Though Can-Am races were falling to conventional cars from Europe, native constructors Chaparral (No. 66, Jim Hall in his 2G) and Autodynamics (No. 1, Sam Posey in the de Dion–suspension Caldwell D7A) were still waving the wings of Yankee innovation. *Harry Kennison*

Floatile afloat: The J-Wax trophy in his lap, Bruce gets a lift from outgoing champ John Surtees (right) and series spokesman Stirling Moss. *Pete Biro*

Center of attention: Going from also-ran to Can-Am domination in one year, Bruce McLaren Motor Racing came back to North America in 1967 with an all-new M6A car, new fuel-injected Chevy motors, and an overall approach learned in Formula One. *Pete Lyons*

Trial of strength: During Las Vegas practice, Hulme (No. 5) had a little dust-up with Hall (No. 66). McLaren (far right) wanted no part of it. *Pete Lyons*

Bigger bird: For 1967, Jim Hall (in helmet) bumped his Chevy engines from 327 to 427 ci and relabeled his Chaparral a 2G. *Pete Lyons*

Moment of glory: Hall's lone Road Runner was fast enough to give the McLaren Kiwi birds some good runs, and twice led Bruce at Riverside.
Claire Lyons McHenry

McLarens weren't there. For all three races so far, Gurney had qualified third fastest with his Lola-Ford, and at Mosport he'd turned a time identical to McLaren's. In each race Dan was holding high positions until his car failed. Penske teammates Mark Donohue and George Follmer also drove other strong-running Lola T70s, as did defending champion John Surtees. Some people with older-style McLarens were quick, too. Another contender was Jim Hall, going solo this year with a big block aluminum Chevy stuffed in one of his Chaparrals, a change that made it a 2G.

Meanwhile, Mario Andretti was in a new Ford factory-backed car called the Honker II, and Sam Posey drove an innovative Caldwell D7. Matich, McKee, Mirage, and Ferrari were other Can-Am carmakers of 1967. Everybody was struggling, though none matched McLaren's M6A.

However, one great thing about racers is that they never give up. And a great thing about racing is, it brings the unexpected. For the mighty McLarens, the second half of the six-race series was much harder work. McLaren himself qualified on pole at Laguna Seca, but Gurney beat Hulme for the outside front row. Denny was having car troubles, and they continued in the race: his Chevy blew. Bruce also had some problems. One was Gurney, who snatched the lead at the start and stayed in front for eight laps. Dan's engine finally let him down again, but that didn't let Bruce off. It was a very hot day, and his M6A's cockpit was an open-pit barbecue. Midrace, he slowed to a crawl on the front straight while a crewman threw a bucket of water over him. On the victory podium, Bruce was suffering from badly sunburned lips.

Riverside was Gurney's home track, and he continued his late-season charge by taking pole away from McLaren. Again, Big Dan led the first part of the race. Again, alas, his Ford grenaded. Hulme also had another bad weekend, going out early with bodywork damage. That left only McLaren to deal with the opposition. And there was opposition. First it was Parnelli Jones in another Lola with a Ford engine, the DOHC powerplant that dominated Indianapolis in those days. This one dominated the Riverside Can-Am for one lap before it melted Jones' tires down.

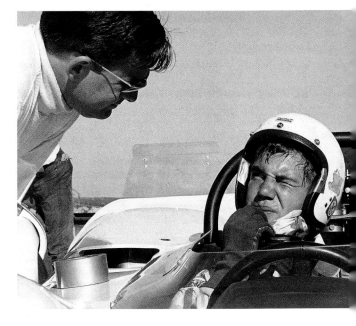

Caldwell D7A. Former driver Ray Caldwell's Autodynamics factory in Marblehead, Massachusetts, built small formula cars. Young Connecticut racer Sam Posey, who had driven an Autodynamics Formula Vee before buying a Can-Am McLaren, agreed to finance Caldwell's conception for a big sports racer. The D7A featured de Dion suspension geometry—"beam axles"(the square-tube truss structure visible surrounding the transaxle)—front and rear to keep the increasingly wider tires of the day flat on the road. On the car's debut at Elkhart Lake (No. 1, exiting the pits past the Chuck Parsons McLaren M1C), it also had a driver-adjustable airfoil similar to the Chaparral's. However, this wing was mounted on the chassis above the engine, not directly on the rear suspension, and the angle was changed through a hand control, not a foot pedal. The ambitious Caldwell showed promise in USRRC racing, but the Can-Am put excessive demands on handling and reliability. After a revised version called the D7B proved no more competitive, Posey turned to a Lola T160 (from the cockpit of which he's conversing with Caldwell in the third picture). *Pete Lyons*

But once McLaren found himself in the lead, he found Hall's Chaparral in his mirrors. For the second year at Riverside, Can-Am fans cheered a duel between the winged white wonder from Texas and a conventional car out of England. This time the fight went all the way to the flag, McLaren getting there first by three seconds. So it was close, but the Kiwi cars now had won five Can-Ams, equaling Lola's 1966 score. The important difference: It was the factory team that had done all the winning, and either McLaren himself or Hulme would take the title.

The Bruce and Denny Show duly moved to the season finale at Las Vegas. There the McLaren luck turned sour. Bruce won pole, but his engine gave out soon after the green flag. Denny had engine trouble both in qualifying and the race. As The Bear coasted to the side of Stardust Raceway, Boss Bruce became Can-Am king.

Of course there was still a race going on. Winning it looked like a lottery. Parnelli Jones was the first leader, until he had transmission trouble. Hall took over, chased by Gurney, but then they too faded. Toward the end, Donohue was heading for his first win, until he ran out of gas. It was the last lap! Mark was in sight of the checker when John Surtees caught him.

As it happened, the past champion was using the same Lola that had won this same race for him the year before. But that gave neither Surtees nor anyone else any illusions. McLaren's all-out effort was the only way to win in the Can-Am.

Chinook Mark 1. George Fejer and brother Rudy, originally from Hungary, become significant players in Canadian racing during the 1960s. The Fejers' short line consisted of four Chinook sports racers, all similar, with space frames stiffened by aluminum paneling and holding Chevy engines, Hewland transmissions, and suspension featuring Fejer-made cast uprights and wheels. Bodywork was said to be copied from a Chaparral slot car model. Here at Mosport's Moss Corner, Nat Adams leads Eppie Wietzes's Ford GT40 en route to 14th and 11th places, respectively. *Dale von Trebra*

Ferrari P3. Ludovico Scarfiotti appeared in two Can-Ams with an open-top P3/P4 (No. 32), a cut-down veteran of European endurance racing entered by U.S. Ferrari importer Luigi Chinetti's NART. Against purpose-built sprinters it was only fast enough to qualify midpack, and though Scarfiotti finished a decent seventh at Bridgehampton, he crashed out at Mosport (where he's seen powersliding out of Moss Corner, ahead of Chuck Parsons' McLaren M1C and 1966 Mosport winner Mark Donohue in a Penske Lola T70.) *Dale von Trebra*

Ferrari P4. In the second half of the season, the Ferrari factory fielded a pair of modified P4s driven by factory F1 stars Chris Amon and Jonathan Williams, but big-torque Can-Am racing was still beyond these admittedly magnificent 4.2-liter, quad-cam V-12s. At Las Vegas, the drivers confer at the pit wall while mechanic Giulio Borsari shows Williams' car to photographer Claire Lyons McHenry. *Pete Lyons*

Other shapes 1967: Matich SR3R. Australian racer Frank Matich tried the series with a neatly purposeful machine powered by Australia's Repco V-8. This was a larger, 4.0-liter version of the Buick-based, overhead-cam engine that won the F1 world championship in 1966 (Jack Brabham) and 1967 (Denny Hulme), but it still wasn't large enough to match the Can-Am's typical 6.0 Chevy. *Bob Tronolone*

McKee Mark 7. In 1961 Indy mechanic Bob McKee accomplished one of the earliest of V-8 swaps into a midengined sports car, the Rodger Ward Cooper-Buick. Five years later, he was a manufacturer of complete cars of his own designs. The McKee Marks 6 and 7 offered the U.S. privateer another domestic choice over English equipment. A strong, pragmatic vehicle, it featured a steel tube space frame incorporating a magnesium front bulkhead, fiberglass bodywork owing some direct ancestry to the Lotus 19, and numerous economical off-the-shelf passenger car parts. That's McKee balanced on one foot at the front of the car. Consulting the driver, Charlie Hayes, who qualified a good 11th on the grid, is TV star and keen racer Dick Smothers. *Pete Lyons*

McKee transaxle: Before you could transplant big power into a little midengined chassis, you had to find some durable way to send it to the road. Not a simple search in 1961, but McKee's solution was hot rodding ingenuity at its best. He cast a housing to take a Ford ring gear/pinion and a limited-slip differential rescued from a junked Mercedes-Benz 300 SL. To the back of that, he bolted a Chevy Corvette 4-speed transmission rotated about 135 degrees so the input shaft could pass alongside the bottom of the ring gear. Then he attached a Halibrand quick-change gearset from the oval speedway world to turn the power flow back toward the differential. McKee transaxles made possible several early big sports racers, including Shelby's King Cobras. *Pete Lyons*

Denny Hulme

HE WAS CALLED "THE BEAR" for his lazy-looking strength and occasionally irascible temperament, but the nickname also could have referred to his scruff-of-the-neck handling of Big Banger race cars. In both respects, the image wasn't the whole picture. Inside, Denny was a genuinely warm person with a great competitive heart who inspired true devotion among his teammates. In a car, he had unusual mechanical sensitivity and could wring astonishing speed out of it without abusing it.

Hulme (he pronounced it as in "hull," using the "m" but the "e" silent) joined fellow New Zealander Bruce McLaren's Can-Am team in 1967, and immediately won the first race in what would become known as the "Bruce and Denny Show" era. He went on to a total of 22 Can-Am wins, more than twice the number achieved by anyone else, and won the whole series in 1968 and 1970. With John Surtees, Hulme was one of the two Can-Am titlists who were also F1 World Champions.

The following material has been synthesized from talks with Denny during vintage events at Watkins Glen in 1990 and again at Laguna Seca in 1992—just two months before his untimely passing.

The Bear—Denis Clive Hulme, Can-Am King, two-time series champion, and winner of 22 races. *Pete Biro*

Now I look back and people say "You were really great." I guess we were. But we didn't think so. At the time it was just Bruce and me and the team having a good time. Yeah, we tried hard. But we tried to make a lot of fun of it as well, and enjoy ourselves. The Can-Am was just a weekend out with the sports cars, as far as I was concerned. I liked the traveling.

What I didn't realize, and I'm only beginning to work it out, I was part of a very historic piece of auto racing in the United States.

There was nothing like the big engines. And that's what the fans thought: "The bigger the better." Yeah. That was neat.

Sometimes in the Can-Am, you didn't seem to be quite as alert and interested as you did at F1 races.

I've got to laugh at that, because in the Can-Am I tried to give people the impression I wasn't interested in anything. Try and make them think, What's he up to today? Is he going to do it or isn't he? Make them think, He's very unpredictable. But certainly, I was really there to give it my best shot.

I didn't really enjoy the press a helluva lot. I thought going to press conferences was a bit of bind. 'Course I realize a lot of those things are wrong now. But I was much happier around the swimming pool at the hotel, and then straight to the circuit and do my thing. Not that I was hiding from the fans or anything like that, but I just wanted to be myself.

What I found in America is that everybody wants to come up and tell you how you should be running your car, or what it's doing around the circuit. But Christ, I was driving the thing. I knew. I had enough problems without everybody telling me what the problems were. These were armchair drivers. Consequently, I just didn't like sitting chewing the fat. I'd sooner get out there and try and work it out.

Bear at play. It's 1969, when McLaren's Bruce and Denny Show was utterly dominant. In later years, the gruff old Hulme let on that he'd really been enjoying himself all along. *Pete Biro*

Whenever Denny wasn't driving hard, he was usually thinking quietly, or maybe absorbed in working on his own car. Unless he was napping. *Pete Lyons*

Hulme

Can-Am cars usually were faster than contemporary F1 cars around the same tracks.

Yes. Just the sheer horsepower. They got from point A to point B much quicker than an F1 car. Because of the power, they had more downforce as well. We could crank on a heap of wing and never mind the drag. But unfortunately they were slightly heavier, particularly when we had a lot of fuel on board, and we didn't understand all the technology. So the F1 car in the slower part of the corner was probably quicker than the Can-Am.

You could be much more sloppy with the Can-Am. We probably weren't, Bruce and I, but if you did goof with the Can-Am, you could make it up the next lap. Because it had the grunt. "Say, I've done a real grotty one here. Now let's get going." F1, you had to be going all the time, you couldn't afford to make one sloppy move.

However, you couldn't toss the Can-Am car at a corner, arrive sideways. They had too much umph. When you cracked the throttle with those old Chevys, you suddenly got 500 horsepower there on tap, instantly. You could only really go around the corner one way. Set up, put the power on the road, and go for it. They were basically set up to understeer all the time, which you could then control with the throttle.

Was it hard to change your mental focus between a Can-Am weekend and a Grand Prix?

Yeah, going back to Grand Prix, you had the world's best drivers to be up against. You knew

Hulme loved the democratic atmosphere at McLaren, where the enthusiastic and gregarious Bruce spent much of his time on the shop floor with the "lads." (From left: Hulme, McLaren, Alec Greaves.) *Tyler Alexander*

you weren't going to be on pole unless you were extremely lucky and had a good day. The intensity of the competition was greater.

But when we left England to come here [for a Can-Am] we knew we'd be on pole, and we had some tricks up our sleeves if anybody got close. We'd carry a little handful of special bits and pieces.

I'm not saying the Americans were dummies, and there were a lot of F1 drivers who did the Can-Am. In fact, half the F1 field was here on a weekend. That was great. I think that's what helped generate the Can-Am into a great series.

Which Can-Am circuit was your favorite?

Oh, I didn't really have a favorite. Elkhart Lake was always nice to go to. I liked Riverside, because you could get up to a good speed. I never liked St. Jovite much, because of that jump. You were always afraid of the front end coming up.

Talk about some of your adversaries. What about Roger Penske Racing and Mark Donohue, who ran one of your old cars against you in 1968?

They were always a threat. Mark was a very capable person in testing and altering cars. He played a lot on skid pads and got a very good handling car on slow corners. Fortunately, all the circuits weren't slow, so it evened out a bit. But Roger was well prepared to spend a dollar and built a very competitive motor car. Luckily, most times we were able to head him off. But Roger was always an enormous threat to us.

So was Jim Hall. I thought he was an excellent driver. Always coming up with new innovations. Jim never had much to say. But when he did, you listened.

He was always very fair, I think, until McLaren put a lot of pressure on getting the sucker thing banned [in 1970]. But I'm always glad that the sucker car was built. It proved something. I don't think Jim was the original innovator, but it certainly worked. It was impressive when they started up the [fan] engine, and you could see the whole car suck down. He was showing a lot of courage with this ugly car, but he was there.

Did the Chaparral's automatic transmission give an advantage?

No. I thought that was a big disadvantage. We knew that we could get him off the line. It always took that automatic a little bit to lock itself into place and get going. We felt if we could get the jump on it at the beginning of the race, we pretty much had him sussed. And he had to carry a lot of weight in extra oil. I think he had 8 or 9 gallons on board just for the transmission.

Chaparral was using the big block Chevy engine in 1967, a year before McLaren.

Yes. He'd got that away from Chevy. Places like Riverside, he could honk down that straight. Then he had the wing that tilted up and down, up and down. We could stay with him in the corner, but that thing was very fast in a straight line. We had to carry the same downforce all the time. He could eliminate a lot of that drag when he was going fast.

Why was Bruce McLaren's team so successful?

Bruce had a very good approach to the Can-Am. Probably better than for Formula One. He really wanted to win every time in the Can-Am. F1 was much more difficult, because you had the Chapmans and Tyrrells, those sort of people, to compete against. Whereas Bruce was very dominant in the Can-Am series, he was king and always wanted to stay king.

An experimental wheel that "looked a million dollars"—before it cracked. *Tyler Alexander*

Hulme

Can-Am cars evolved quickly in those days. At Bridgehampton 1968, Bruce in his new M8A spares a glance at Candy DaMota's M1C, the customer-model McLaren of just a year before. Hulme said that by comparison to the narrow, low-downforce early cars, which had light steering, the wide, wedge-shaped "flying aircraft carriers" were hard work. *Pete Lyons*

The beauty of Bruce was that we'd go testing and do anything. He'd come home with a piece of paper, sketch it out, and say, "Make it." It was made the following morning, almost.

But there was no hierarchy. It was the simplicity within the team; you didn't need a committee meeting. If you had an idea, you told Bruce, or you said to Teddy [Mayer] or Tyler [Alexander], "Why isn't this or that tried?" Or if the mechanics could see a better way of doing something, they did it, virtually without asking a question.

I think in some of the other teams, the mechanics were there as pushers and shovers and changers of engines. It wasn't the case at McLaren. Generally, it was a happy team. It was just a young team that grew up that way. We didn't really have any corporate structure. There was no separate office as such for Bruce. The mechanics had liberty to go and see him whenever they wanted. But he spent more time down there talking to them on the floor.

So it was really an excellent arrangement. Nobody was a stranger to one another. If you didn't

Bruce at work at Goodwood testing the M8B, the perfectly developed McLaren that Hulme called his favorite. *Tyler Alexander*

agree with Bruce, you could say something. He was the type of person who didn't really take offense. He listened. I think that's what made the team work so well, and why we were able to come back every week with something a little smarter.

Also, the amount of time we went testing. We went testing every Wednesday or Thursday at Goodwood. No matter what happened in Formula One, no matter whether we were in America, we had to be down at Goodwood on the following Wednesday and drive a donkey car over there, learn something or test something. We just cranked the miles up. We got those cars perfect, so when we came racing, we were ready to go racing. We weren't ready to go testing.

Did you personally have any input to the design of the car?

Nope. Nothing whatsoever.

One of the mechanics once told me that they built a throttle linkage, and you came through the shop and put all your muscle on it and it broke. You said, "Make it stronger," and walked away.

[Laughing] Well, it was never any fun going to the circuit and thinking, Geesh, this is going to snap. I'd go and sit in a car and put all the weight I could on a brake pedal or something to see if I could break it or bend it.

We had a spate of the wheels cracking. We built spun magnesium wheels for the Can-Am car. They looked a million dollars, all nice and wide. Went down to Goodwood, we did one and a half laps, and the bloody things fell apart. We turned them into coffee tables the next day.

There were quite a few things that went wrong secretly. When I joined Bruce in 1967, I went to the McLaren factory, and I couldn't fit into the prototype M6. So they had to build my car longer between the wheels. Then Alister Caldwell came along into the team, and they told him to make some things for my car. When he came to fit them, there was a two-inch gap. They said, "Oh gosh, we forgot to tell you. We made Denis' car two inches longer.'

The amount of work behind the scenes must have been staggering.

When you look back, no team had the capability of McLaren when you think what we ran. We were building Indy cars, Can-Am cars, F1 cars, F2, F5000; just doing it in everything. With a fairly small team. I think we got up to 60 at the maximum personnel. They have 150 or something there now, just to run F1 cars. I know it's more sophisticated, but that's the case. Maybe we all just worked harder.

We had, I think, good designers, good engineers. Robin Herd did the first one, and Gordon Coppock came along, and it progressed from there. The cars were simple and quick. They turned out to be a unique motor car, an expensive motor car, now, if you wish to purchase one. I wish I'd collected every one. Teddy was screaming to give them away, sometimes, at the end of each year. But little did we know. We were going to get a new one, a better one, next year. Who wanted the old heap of junk?

Was Bruce just that intensely driven? Did he think motor racing 24 hours a day?

I don't think he ever stopped thinking about it, but he didn't talk about it all day long. Teddy certainly did. Teddy stored it all in his head, and he can probably tell you all the settings still. I think Teddy would yak away about motor racing all day, but I think every now and again Bruce wanted to go and do something else, maybe water skiing.

What were the important things Teddy Mayer brought to it?

Coordinating the team. Teddy pieced it all together. Bruce would have a flash and say, "Let's do that, that, that, and that." Teddy's thing would be to go and make it happen.

Tyler Alexander?

Tyler kept the team on an even keel. If anybody was becoming a little headstrong, he'd tell 'em. If he thought Teddy or Bruce was maybe going off on a tangent somewhere, he'd have his say. He kept the team contained in what he thought was the most obvious direction to be going. Tyler was able to sit back and say, "That ain't right. Why don't we all think about this?" So he had very good footing.

Then, he had the engineering ability to say, "The gearbox is not strong enough. We'd better sort something out. We need it tomorrow."

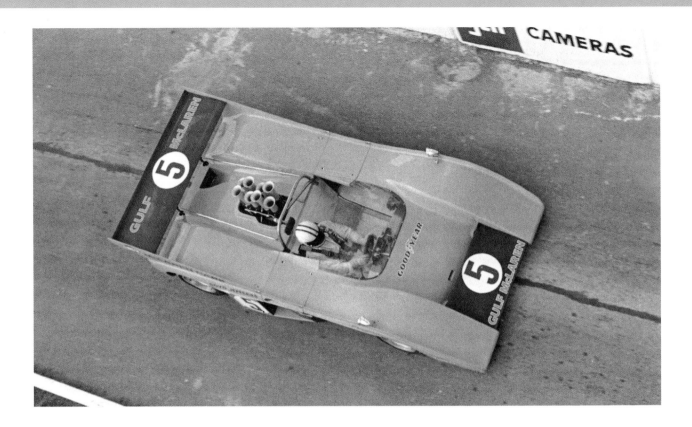

In 1972, after four years with M8-series cars that were essentially evolutions of one design, McLaren stepped up to the Porsche Panzer challenge with the M20. Even though Denny never raced with the turbo engine the car was made for, he was almost fast enough. *Pete Lyons*

Everybody respected Tyler and what he said. He'd been around for a long time.

Your mechanics never stopped working.

Jimmy Stone, Cary Taylor, Alec Greaves . . . . There was more than that, of course, but we were quite a small team. But all of them had the ability that, if you wanted a square wheel, they'd rush away and make you a square wheel. They would just fly into the problem. Cars would all come to pieces, and it was all put right.

Virtually all the cars you saw on Sunday were different cars than what we had on Saturday, other than the tub. We just had so many spares—new ring and pinion, brand-new clutch, new pads. If on Saturday afternoon I wanted a new third gear, when it came to Sunday, I didn't have that same third gear even though it was new the day before. They'd put in all new stuff. Sunday morning it was like a brand-new car.

The things were fairly highly stressed and the McLaren team would spend an awful lot of money just on the maintenance side of it to be sure we didn't break down. It was probably one of the very first teams to put that kind of effort in. We needed to finish one-two to pay the bills. Otherwise, we were buried. There was no great big bank full of money. The prize money was what the team lived on from race to race.

We didn't want for anything. We had plenty of bodies and chassis and tubs. But they're always expensive. We were running then on a tight budget. We sold the pace car and the winner's circle car, which I think we did win one weekend at Riverside. It was quite a good payday, but we needed all that. We never kept anything. We sold the gold bars we won at Edmonton on Monday morning. We went down to the bank, cashed them up, pressed on, and paid the hotel bill.

You had more sponsors than anyone else in those days.

Yes, all the people whose decals were on the side of the car helped enormously. I don't think there was any big fund of money from them, but clutches and brakes all came F.O.C.—"Free Of Charge." Of course, we were going through a lot of that sort of stuff, and it was very valuable help.

I can now see that the Americans must have been really worried that there was a bunch of Kiwis over here, those orange cars, snapping up the money. There was an untold amount of energy and effort put in by some big companies over here to blow us away. It looked like they were beating their heads against a brick wall.

Porsche, of course, actually did the number on us. We were very disappointed that we got blitzed, but we couldn't sustain the pressure from Porsche with the budget they had, which was absolutely enormous. They were consuming on a weekend what we'd spend in a year on brakes, for example. We just couldn't see the light of day, that it was going to be very profitable for McLaren to carry on to try and beat the Porsches. So it got flagged.

I'm sure in hindsight we could have done a helluva lot better. We weren't very far away. The Porsche was a heavy motorcar, and had we been able to get another 50 or 60 horsepower from the Chevrolet, we would have been right back with them again.

It was all learning. Think: Even with flat bottoms in F1 they find they can generate all the downforce in the world, but we could have been doing that. We had a beautiful area of flat bottom underneath the car to work on. And we could be up to probably 20-inch diameter rims on the back and 25 inches wide. You'd get a longer footprint, obviously, and a stiffer sidewall as well. It would stop those old girls from wobbling with the big fat tires we had. And with the carbon brakes of today. . . .

Can you imagine? Today, with the electronic ignition and engine management and the fuel injection, those same Chevrolets that we had would easily get 1,600 horsepower. And if you put a quad cam and four valves in it—God! They would be absolutely unreal machines, fabulous machines, the ultimate race car.

Indy champion Parnelli Jones forces the Indy-engined Lola to the Can-Am fore at Las Vegas 1966. It was his Midget training coming out, he says.
Claire Lyons McHenry

Parnelli Jones

RUFUS PARNELLI JONES came from the rough 'n' tumble world of the USAC bull rings, and won numerous midget, sprint, and stock car races besides his great triumph, the 1963 Indianapolis 500. Later on Parnelli would become a champion in Trans-Am road racing—and in the off-road Baja 1000 too—but in 1964 he had very little sports car experience when Carroll Shelby asked him to try a King Cobra (Cooper-Ford) at Riverside. The story conveys the casually raw flavor of those early days

Of course Shelby was a Goodyear distributor and I was a Firestone distributor, so I asked, "What are we going to do about the tires?" He said, "Well, you can run whatever's best." I said, "OK, you got a deal."

It was funny. I got out there the first day and we ran the Goodyears, then I put the Firestones on and they were better. Well Shelby wasn't there, he took off somewhere, and the next day his managers, Al Dowd and Peyton Cramer, said, "We had a little meeting last night and decided we're going to run the Goodyear tires." I said, "I just had a meeting and decided I'm not going to drive the car."

So I walked off. They grabbed me and said, "Well, would you qualify the car?" I said, "On Firestone tires?" They said yeah, so I qualified the car third quick [to Dan Gurney, Lotus-Ford, and Bruce McLaren, McLaren-Oldsmobile]. There were two other King Cobras, and they were back eighth or ninth or something. At that point they figured they had to protect their Ford interests as well, so they decided to let me run the race.

If you remember, we used to run heat races on Saturday and then the 200-miler on Sunday. Saturday, I kept spinning out. I'd catch back up, spin out. I said to myself that night, "Hey, Jones. If you'd just quit spinning out you'd win the race." So the next day I made a commitment that I wasn't going to spin the car, and anyway I took off and won the race. It was kind of like my first sports car race.

A week later at Laguna Seca I broke a wheel going into the first turn down there and wound up on top of the bank and skint my knee up.

Two years later, when the first Can-Am series moved out west to Laguna Seca, the Lola importer, John Mecom, put you into a T-70 with a small block Ford engine.

I think the very first practice the engine blew up. Somehow Roger Penske loaned us a Chevrolet engine, so we put it in overnight. Of course we had missed qualifying, and we had to run in the back of the consolation race. I won that hands down. That put me in the back of the first 100-mile heat race.

The Chevrolet oil pan was a little deeper than the Ford and it was rubbing on the race track. Probably up in the Corkscrew. I wore a hole in it, so they black-flagged me. We welded up the pan and put a couple of turns in the spring, raised it up a little bit. We had to start dead last again in the second 100.

I started motoring up through the guys, and I got up to fourth. The two Chaparrals, Phil Hill and Jim Hall, were leading the race, and John Surtees was running third in another Lola. When I caught him he started blocking me, coming lower than he normally would into the hairpin and also up under the bridge. The Chaparrals were starting to get away from us. I thought, "I'm better off to act like I can't pass him for a few laps." Finally he got out wider, where he should have been, and I dove underneath him under the bridge, and we rubbed sides and he went off the track. Of course he was quite mad at me . . .

Didn't he come after you later?

No, no, he did not. He just "voiced" me a little bit. He didn't like my driving style.

Anyway, then I caught the Chaparrals and passed them both in the same lap, and won the race [that second heat, for 21st overall]. After I had passed them the yellow flag came out, but I had it all over 'em. I was just running quicker. Well, I had to be, coming from dead last. And I was handling well and was really working well.

After that they said the Chevy engine was all tired, because it had been used in a race before I got it, and so they were going to build me a nice big fresh engine for Riverside. They did, and we never could get the thing running worth a darn. [chuckling] So you have good days and bad days.

How did the Lola feel compared to the Cooper?

The Cooper was good in its day. They were both good-handling cars, I never had any complaints about either one, but the Lola was a step up. Basically they felt the same. It's just that you could run quicker in the Lola.

What about that Ford Indy engine you had for the Can-Am in 1967?

Well, Mecom had George Bignotti as his mechanic at Indianapolis when Graham Hill won, and so they decided to put a four-cam Indy engine in the Lola and they wanted me to drive it.

We had a lot of struggling problems the first two or three races with it, because they were trying to run it on gasoline and it had been set up to run on alcohol. On gasoline we had real problems with vapor locking, it would heat the fuel. We finally got it handled, I mean at Riverside, we were running right up front.

You led the race for a lap. The engine finally blew, but how did it compare to the pushrod engines?

I just compare 'em as how I am in competition with the other cars. It was good. It was a high-rev engine, because it was a four-cammer, and it probably didn't have as much torque as the Chevy did. But it had a lot of top-end horsepower.

At Las Vegas I was leading it going away, and all of a sudden the gearshift fell off in my hand.

You gained a few positions before the start there.

Well. . . . When you come out of midgets and sprint cars, where it's 100 percent for 30 laps, you learn to be very aggressive at the start. If you see an opening you go for it.

I guess it's kind of like a quarter horse against a thoroughbred. That quarter horse comes out running as hard as he can run. The thoroughbred paces himself. I've never been very good at pacing myself. I don't know how in the hell I ever won the Baja 1000. [laughing] But I had Bill Stroppe with me, beating on me and slowing me down.

A hard-bitten veteran of some tough leagues, P.J. might have been a bit more of a competitor than the genteel SCCA expected in its Challenge Cup. *Ozzie Lyons*

1968: Bigger Bangers

The Teams Embrace Big Block Power

After showing everybody else how to go Can-Am racing in 1967, this time McLaren failed to follow its own book. The champions did build a fresh car again and joined the year's big tech trend to big-inch Chevrolet power. But delays caused by bad English weather, as well as a busier time for the team in F1, kept it from exterminating all the new-car bugs in the McLaren M8A before its first race.

What saved the Kiwis was the inability of any of their would-be rivals to do any better. Denny Hulme and Bruce McLaren qualified one-two for Elkhart Lake, just as they had the year before. This time they finished that way, though Hulme's aluminum 7.0 Chevy clattered under the checker on seven cylinders and zero oil pressure.

At Bridgehampton, McLaren's problems worsened. While the caramel-colored M8As again started at the front, both cars had engine troubles in practice, then both blew in the race. Jim Hall mounted a stiff challenge; in fact, he put his aging Chaparral 2G up front for five glorious laps. Then its Chevrolet faltered too. Donohue won with his 1968 production-model McLaren M6B—and a reliable version of the big Chevy.

Many teams would have been helpless to change their power package this late in the season, but McLaren's investment in an engine shop of its own really paid off now. In the two weeks following the Bridgehampton debacle the problem was solved, and Canada's Edmonton hosted a revival of the Bruce and Denny Show. At the half-way point, the season seemed to be as good as over.

But then it rained in California. On race day at Laguna Seca—"dry lake"—the Big Banger sports racers looked like hydroplane boats. All except for one little old

Denny Hulme (1968 McLaren M8A) crests a Bridgehampton rise with Jim Hall (Chaparral 2G) giving chase. *Pete Lyons*

Still fast: Though the winged Road Runner was three years old, Hall put it ahead of the brand-new big-engined McLaren M8As at Bridgehampton for five splendid laps. *Pete Lyons*

Hot-rodded special: Hall's 2G was originally one of the lightweight, elegant 2Es of 1966 with 100 more cubic inches and much fatter "meats." *Pete Lyons*

Full stride: This year the Bruce and Denny Show only took four races out of the six, but privateers put the McLaren brand up front the other two times. Here at the end of Riverside's mile-long back straight, Laguna Seca winner John Cannon (No. 62 M1B) lets the boss sweep by. *Pete Lyons*

McLaren M1B, on which crafty Canadian John Cannon had put a set of Firestone rain tires intended for F1 cars. Starting 15th on the grid, Cannon won by a full lap over Denny Hulme. He passed a miserable Bruce McLaren two times.

Bruce got his grin back at Riverside, where the weather was dry and the M8B was the hottest thing on the track. The defending Can-Am champ qualified on pole and led every lap to take his first win of the year. Meanwhile, Hulme, the series leader, came in fifth after busting his bodywork for the second year in a row at Riverside. Cannon managed an honorable sixth place, earning himself one more championship point.

Las Vegas in 1968 had a first-turn shunt almost as bad as Mosport's in 1966. Starting from his fourth pole of the year, McLaren somehow came together with sixth-fastest Mario Andretti (Lola T160-Ford). Hall's Chaparral, in third grid place, was also caught up. All three temporarily vanished in an explosion of desert dust and stones but were able to continue. Not so lucky were some behind, including Chris Amon and his brand new Ferrari 612P; its 12 throttles jammed with dirt, it never moved past the first turn of its first race.

Nobody was hurt in that incident, but later in the race Hall rammed the back of Lothar Motschenbacher (McLaren M6B-Chevy). The Chaparral flew straight up, slammed down hard, and split in half. The resulting severe leg injuries ended Hall's competitive driving career. Safely ahead of all the day's dramas, Hulme won his third Can-Am of the year, and his first Can-Am Challenge Cup trophy. McLaren, his M8A battered and also brakeless by the end, finished sixth in the race, but second in the championship.

The McLaren team dominated the series again, but others did put up a fight. Jim Hall's Chaparral 2G may have been getting old, but it was faster than ever. Hall qualified third three

Pinstriped preview: Mark Donohue, racing here at Riverside, won the 1968 Bridgehampton Can-Am in Roger Penske's immaculate McLaren M6B. Four years later, the pair joined Porsche to blow McLaren out of the series. *Pete Lyons*

times, second once, set fastest race lap another time, and briefly led at Bridgehampton. Mark Donohue's win there was a matter of lasting the distance, but he did qualify his older-style McLaren on the second row five times and took third in the points.

At various times, too, strong performances were turned in by Mario Andretti (Ford-powered Lola T70 and T160), George Follmer (T70-Ford), Dan Gurney (Ford-powered, modified McLaren M6B known as the "McLeagle"), Lothar Motschenbacher (M6B with Ford and Chevy engines), Chuck Parsons (Lola T160-Chevy), Sam Posey (Lola T160-Chevy), Peter Revson (M6B-Ford), Skip Scott (T160-Chevy), John Surtees(T160-Chevy), and Jerry Titus (M6B-Chevy).

There was plenty of talent in the Can-Am. What was lacking was commitment to constructing new, McLaren-matching machinery. To raise the stakes, in 1969 the series would grow from 6 events to 11.

Railbirds: Hulme (left) cocks an ear as Donohue (middle) takes a punchline from McLaren. *Pete Biro*

Bear: He could be gruff, but winning brought out Denny Hulme's happy side. Twice the series champion, he had over twice as many Can-Am victories as anyone else. *Ray Jeanotte*

Can-Am champ: Hulme put his big, heavy boot into McLaren's big block M8A and maintained the Kiwi Can-Am momentum with three wins and the series title. *Pete Lyons*

Stern Chase: Bridgehampton winner Donohue (foreground) simply had to outlast Hulme's McLaren and Hall's Chaparral. *Pete Lyons*

Pure power: McLaren engine man Lee Muir screws stacks onto the big aluminum-block 427 Chevy. *Pete Lyons*

Rainmaster: At Laguna Seca, John Cannon put his old McLaren M1B onto rain tires and splashed to victory lane. *Pete Biro*

Two years after first flying its flipper wing at Bridgehampton, Chaparral was still the only constructor taking full advantage of the invention. *Pete Lyons*

Stardust Can-Am, Las Vegas, 1968: Jim Hall (No. 66 Chaparral 2G), Dan Gurney (No. 48 Lola T160), Bruce McLaren (No. 4 McLaren M8A), Sam Posey (No. 1 Lola T160), George Follmer (No. 16 Lola T70), Peter Revson (No. 52 McLaren M6B), Denny Hulme (No. 5 McLaren M8A). *Pete Biro*

Terry T10-Chevrolet. A sleek-looking sister of a Ford-engined vehicle that was built in 1967 for Carroll Shelby's Cobra team by English designer Len Terry, this Chevy version was no more successful. Driver Nick de Courville didn't make the field here at Riverside, the car's only Can-Am appearance in 1968. However, in 1970 Skeeter McKitterick did qualify the car at the same track, and what's more he finished the race in 14th place. *Bob Tronolone*

Hero worship: In the 1960s, every boy wanted to grow up to be Dan Gurney, even Bobby Unser's Bobby Jr. *Pete Lyons*

Denny Hulme, Can-Am Champion 1968 (McLaren M8A). *Harry Kennison*

Burnetts. One of those remarkable individuals who insist on building their own race cars, Stan Burnett was a machinist from Seattle who used bodywork from Huffaker Genies for his pair of small block Chevy-powered Mark 2 specials. However, he crafted everything else himself—tube frames, suspension parts, even the transaxles. He and friend Don Jenson raced these for several years. Jenson (No. 0) is shown in the rain at Laguna Seca 1968 with winner Cannon's No. 62 McLaren M1B and the No. 34 George Follmer Lola T70. Meanwhile Burnett built a single new Mark 3 for himself, using some of his original Mark 2 chassis, but modifying the rear to take a big block Chevy. This time, he also made his own body, along more modern McLaren M6B lines. That's him in the No. 64 at Riverside, making way for fellow American constructor Jim Hall (No. 66 Chaparral 2G) as they both tuck into Turn 9 behind Jim Paul's McLaren M1C. *Pete Lyons*

Tyler Alexander

HIS NAME WASN'T ON THE CARS, nor did he back the business, but this American's role in McLaren's success cannot be overstated. Looking back, Tyler tends to describe his contribution simply as "work," and he is indeed a renowned workaholic in that epic of endless toil that is motor racing. But he put in so much more than mere effort. Passion, nerve, intelligence, mechanical talent, engineering inventiveness, inflexible perfectionism, relentlessly competitive spirit, good humor; everything about him helped nourish the team. Joining McLaren along with Teddy Mayer, Tyler quickly became both a devoted fan and close personal friend of Bruce—they shared a house for years. The former aviation mechanic helped build the very first McLarens, served as crew chief (and much more) throughout the Can-Am era, and became a

A close friend of Bruce McLaren as well as a key "Kiwi," American aviation mechanic Tyler Alexander (left, with Bruce in his M8A at Bridgehampton 1968) helped the New Zealander build a small sports car team into a great international organization. *Pete Lyons*

company director. Although the McLaren organization has since changed hands and evolved beyond recognition, he remains a key part of its Formula One team as Special Projects Manager.

I remember a lot of good things. There was an enormous amount of hard work. A lot of fun. Also, there was a huge amount of satisfaction in that we were doing something. I remember saying to Bruce on several occasions, "Son of a bitch, we're actually on our way here, aren't we. We ought to keep at this!"

The stuff we did was pretty basic when you look back on it, but we did a lot of things that other people weren't doing. No one told us we couldn't, so you just did them. Mounting the engine in the back of the car with no chassis around it; how do you do that? Well, get a hacksaw and cut the back off the chassis.

Bruce wasn't too daunted by any of that stuff. Some of it worked, some of it didn't. Although he wanted to keep the thing basically simple, he was also into anything new. He would draw on the back of a fag [cigarette] packet and fling it on the table and say, "I'll be back next week. See what you can do with this."

McLaren was a trained engineer and a self-made racing driver, who drove a factory F1 Cooper to victory in the first-ever U.S. Grand Prix in 1959. So much did he enjoy racing in America—and winning dollars—that he became a regular on the U.S. and Canadian professional sports car circuit. At first he ran Coopers like the four-cylinder, Coventry Climax-powered Monaco he's pondering here. *Pete Biro*

Bruce must have been the kind of guy you'd work 100-hour weeks for.

Yeah. He had this tremendous charisma. I remember somebody asking what I was doing, and I said, "I don't know. There's this funny guy with the short leg [Bruce suffered Perthe's disease as a

When Bruce decided to set up his own factory, he started with Roger Penske's infamous Zerex Special—an ex-F1 Cooper-Climax turned into a sports car—and had Tyler Alexander install an Oldsmobile V-8. The hastily completed Anglo-American hot rod won its first time out, here at Mosport in 1964. *Pete Lyons*

After Tyler (holding flag) and Colin Beanland (middle) swapped the 1965 McLaren M1B's original Olds for a Chevy between race weekends, Bruce thanked them with a brisk victory lap at St. Jovite. *Lionel Birnbom*

The Chevy swap almost done, Tyler stepped back in the borrowed Massachusetts garage and picked up his camera. Although by 1965 other constructors had moved to monocoque chassis, notably sports car rival Lola, McLaren was sticking with a simple, straightforward space frame. *Tyler Alexander*

child] who seems to know quite a bit about motor racing, and I think perhaps I'd better tag along and see what happens." Really, those were the words!

The whole thing was so different than anything that exists now. Things were done because there was a person who was the driving force, like Colin Chapman at Lotus, and Bruce was the driving force behind McLaren. A man with a lot of drive. He tended to be pushy. He was full of ideas all the time. Too many of them sometimes, but he was certainly full of ideas.

Was Bruce particularly good at test driving, would you say?

Um . . . in hindsight, he was good at testing, but he was also very capable of making what he wanted to work, work. I remember a scenario with some low, offset wheels for the Can-Am car that he reckoned were fantastic and made the steering lighter. About the third race, Hulme had been quicker than him all the time, and Bruce put the other wheels back on, and of course the car was quicker. Hulme said he could have told you that.

Certainly a lot of his success can be put down to his insistence on testing. He was adamant that we test all the time.

Bruce liked to test new cars before the bodywork was put on. I guess the idea was to first develop the handling in terms of what is now called mechanical grip?

Exactly. Yes, he was into that. How effective it was, I don't know. Without the bodywork you couldn't drive it very quick anyway. But I don't think we realized that then.

Eoin Young, author of McLaren!, has written of testing at Goodwood, and then four of you would drive back to the shop discussing it.

Yep. That was a standard scenario. Argue and fight and bullshit all the way back. Bruce driving, turning around talking to us in the back seat.

The team was only a few people, in the beginning, and you guys all did everything. I even saw you personally sweep floors.

We did, exactly. Basically, there was a couple of us that worked on each car. There was a guy that sort of fiddled around with the engines, and I fiddled around with the engines as well. Certainly the direction came from Bruce and from Teddy Mayer, who I suppose was the Team Manager. Teddy and I were the two Ugly Americans, and the rest were New Zealanders, with a few English thrown in.

Work—that's what Alexander says he remembers most. That's because he did so much. Here, late Saturday night before race day at Las Vegas 1967, Tyler (far right) rebuilds the Hewland transaxle of Bruce's M6A. His hollow-eyed fellows are engine man Gary Knutson (left), who with Alexander developed this small block Chevy's highly effective fuel-injection system, "Beanie" Beanland (in cockpit) and Mike "Charlie Chins" Underwood. Unfortunately, all their toil would go for naught—both team cars failed for the first time in this final race. *Pete Lyons*

Tell me about Teddy and his contribution.

Well, he was financially very supportive of the company. In fact, probably the thing would not have existed if it were not for him putting his own money in. Whether it was a lot or a little, I don't know, but I know it was there, and it was there on several occasions.

It was mostly Bruce and Bruce's charisma that generated the outside money—what there was of it, and there wasn't very much. Teddy followed it up and obviously did the contractual side of things.

You reckon without Teddy it would never have even gotten off the ground?

No, that's not fair to say. We were going ahead and doing things before Teddy actually appeared on the scene. There was a company

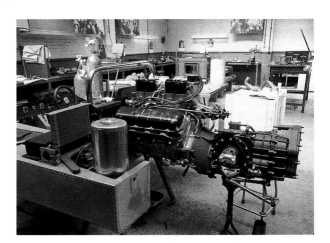

McLaren's first aluminum monocoque sports car chassis was riveted and bonded together for the M6A in 1967. The forks at the rear (right) were to embrace the 359-ci iron-block Chevy engine. These were literally lopped off to make the following year's prototype M8A (second picture), in which the big aluminum 427 was incorporated as a stressed part of the structure. As was his practice, Bruce first tested this vehicle sans aerodynamics to get a feel for the basic "mechanical" handling. *Tyler Alexander*

called Bruce McLaren Motor Racing in place that Teddy was part of, but he didn't come to England for some time.

He just made it more viable. In fact he wrote the check out to buy the Zerex car. Teddy and I were in Stowe, Vermont, when Bruce called and said, "I've got this deal to run a few races, and I think we should buy this car from (John) Mecom. What do you guys think?"

I've heard that Teddy tended to get too much into technical areas.

Um, that would be a fair criticism. The problem is that Teddy's very clever and very bright.

There were fights between him and Bruce all the time. Both were quite headstrong, and Teddy wanted to do things his way, and Bruce wanted to do them his way. Well, that's normal in motor racing.

Tell me about Denny Hulme.

Denny? He was certainly hard to get to know, but when you did get to know him, he really was a lovely guy. A genuine nice guy. Quite a lot of fun. Affable. Likable. Kind of moody. Bit of a strange guy, but interesting. Actually had a lot of good ideas.

Was pretty quick in the car when he wanted to be. I don't really know how quick he was in the end.

I remember a very rude comment as far as how quick he was. We were at Goodwood testing, and Jochen Rindt was there with an F1 car, and he said, "You're never going to find out how quick the car is with those two characters driving it." Referring to Bruce and Denny. Unfortunately, Rindt was very quick. I think he suspected that our car wasn't bad, because otherwise I can't see why he would have made the comment. But that always stuck in the back of my head, that unless you've got the quickest guy driving the car, you don't know where you are. That holds true to this day.

Denny was quite quick and able to run with those guys, but he was no Rindt or Stewart. Those guys would do it every day, day in and day out, every hour. Yet, some days he would be every bit as quick as them. I think it was the mood he was in. You never knew. Once in a while Hulme would surprise the hell out of you.

He said the thing felt all right and he'd just have a bit of a go.

There are stories of him destruct-testing things.

Yep! (laughs) There was the classic scene at Laguna Seca where he bent a brake pedal over his knee. I think he'd actually broken his, and this was a spare one. And he said . . . well, the consensus was, it wasn't strong enough.

I remember he threw a roll of tape at "Top Cat" somewhere. One of those big rolls of tank-tape had been left in the cockpit of the Can-Am car. He came by and pulled over next to the pit wall and threw it at the guy holding the signal board. Tore it out of his hands.

He was an interesting character.

In the aftermath of Bruce's death, people were saying that Denny was the tower of strength holding the team together.

Oh, he was, for sure. Denny did everything humanly possible. Certainly everybody looked up to him. His hands were still bleeding and screwed up from Indianapolis. He did an unbelievable job.

And I think so did Gurney. To be quite honest, Dan helped enormously. Maybe he didn't

As the team grew, Bruce and Tyler remained close. At Edmonton 1969, the driver works his own throttles by hand as the crew chief presses the starter button. Conservative McLaren had finally embraced the rear wing principle for the M8B. *Pete Lyons*

realize what he was doing, but he helped carry the thing and kept everybody pumped up. He won the races for us. If we'd have had somebody else driving the car in those first few races, I think it might have finished the thing off.

What was Gurney like as a driver?

He's another classic character. He obviously had an enormous amount of talent. I really like him.

A funny guy. Complete fiddler. At Mosport, must have been the first race, seems like Vince Higgins and I changed springs on the car 50 times. I can remember saying to Dan, "There's only about 15 minutes left in practice and we're only third or fourth quickest." And he said, "Oh, shit. I guess I'd better do a time, hadn't I?" Of course, he put it on pole. When it came time to go, he just got in it and went. Didn't matter what the setup was.

Peter Revson.

Revvie and I were good friends. He was doing a hell of a job, just getting better and better. I don't know that he was any Jackie Stewart in natural ability, but he was rapidly making up for it by being very bold, and he was starting to have more confidence in himself. I don't think at that stage there was anyone that could drive a Can-Am car, an Indy car, and a Formula One car as quick as Revson. He drove all three very well. I don't think there was anyone in that same league with him.

If we got the chassis right, he was as quick as anybody in the Indy Car. We had unbelievably bad reliability in the Indy car, because we were stupid, or inexperienced, I guess it's called. But when the thing was right, Revvie was on pole and led the races. There were guys that were quicker in F1, but he won a couple of F1 races. And he certainly won a bunch of Can-Am races.

That Zerex car was Roger Penske's old Cooper special. Bruce was a fan of small, light, agile cars, but you replaced the little four-cylinder Coventry Climax engine with an Oldsmobile V-8. Did Bruce have to be persuaded to make that swap?

Even in 1969, when the winged McLaren M8Bs won all 11 Can-Ams, the Kiwis experienced enough trouble to keep them busy. During practice at Riverside, Bruce suddenly appeared at the back door into the pits, asking for help from Tyler and defending Can-Am champion Denny Hulme. The reason was hard to hide: a lunched Chevy 430. *Pete Lyons*

Alexander

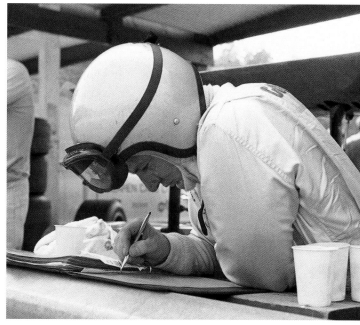

Bruce was serious and scientific about his motor racing, but he made sure to have fun at it too. (Pictures taken at Elkhart Lake and Bridgehampton 1969.) *Pete Lyons*

No, he had to persuade us. It was his idea. He left a wire mock-up and an engine on a cherry picker hanging over the back of the car and said, "I'm off to Spa. Put this in."

We managed to get the car to Goodwood somehow for about an hour of testing. I think it went from there almost straight to the airport. Mosport was the first time it had an Oldsmobile engine in it. We won that race.

We kept the Olds engines for a while. Bruce could qualify well if he could run on his own. But in the race he'd be lapping some of those other characters that weren't particularly quick who had gutsy Chevrolet engines, and he'd be held up for laps.

And anyway, the progress with these various Chevrolet things was going forward quite rapidly. We were starting to strain the old Oldsmobile, trying to run it a bit faster, and it just wouldn't deal with it any more. We were getting out-gunned.

I think it finally dawned on him at St. Jovite that, hey, we're doing the wrong thing here. Then Colin Beanland and I brought the car back to Hingham, Massachusetts [Tyler's hometown], where some friends of mine had basically a wooden shed garage. A crate came from Traco's with a Chevrolet engine in it, and a note that said, "Put this in and I'll see you guys at St. Jovite in two weeks." We did, and we won the race with it.

Bruce took [us] around on the victory lap, and on the back straightaway he said, "About here's where the Oldsmobile stopped pulling. Watch this!" The Chevrolet just kept accelerating. Huge difference.

You mentioned McLaren doing things other teams weren't; what comes to your mind as major evolutionary steps you took?

One of the biggest steps was putting fuel injection on the Chevrolet engine in 1967. We used a Mickey Thompson cross-ram manifold for Weber carburetors and a Lucas metering unit. Mostly that was done by Gary Knutson, with me working with him. I remember running it on the dyno at Alan Mann's to sort out the fuel mixture cam. We actually had control of the fuel, as little as we knew about it in those days, but obviously it worked very well. Needless to say everybody else began to use the stuff a year later, so we really had a big jump on everybody.

Faced with Bruce's death in 1970, his team was determined to press on in a way that would do honor to his legacy. At Mosport, Tyler (right) and Teddy Mayer brief Dan Gurney. Listening in is Fred Nething, crew chief for privateer Gary Wilson. *Lionel Birnbom*

somewhere bumped into Billy Reynolds, I think that was his name. I remember going to somebody's mansion somewhere to talk about it. The development program was between Reynolds, Chevrolet, and us. It was a very good scenario. Other than the financial help that they gave us, they helped develop a lot of things.

For them, at McLaren Engines in Michigan, we did a Vega engine program that was a blatant disaster. They'd blow up all the time.

How much help did you get from Chevrolet?

I'm not sure that's something we should be talking about. Um . . . they helped. They certainly helped in a technical respect, helped to get us out of problems. They helped with getting parts made, and they made stuff available to us at friendly prices. Because we did other things for them. We did a lot of durability running of other engines, and other projects as well.

Bruce and John DeLorean had a pretty good relationship. Whenever I went over there to Chevrolet R&D, the Tech Center in Warren, DeLorean used to come down to the lobby and get you. Quite amusing, really.

I don't remember the exact details, but there would have been a McLaren Corvette road car, a rolloff from the Can-Am thing. We built a couple of prototypes [the McLaren M6GT]. Bruce was very keen to do it.

McLaren cars had a distinctive style of design, very simple, very sturdy.

That was Bruce. Maybe it's because he drove the things himself. No one was really into stressing the stuff properly, so you just made it butch, you know?

Later on, when we hired Gary back from Chaparral, he brought lots of stuff that he had been involved with at Hall's. It helped us just upgrade and sanitize the cars, for sure, because he was exposed to the stuff and we weren't in England.

We learned some things from the Ford people. We were some of the first people to run wider wheels with Goodyear's wider tires. We played around with the brakes and things. There wasn't a lot of stuff to play around with.

We tested a wing on a Can-Am car at Goodwood quite early on, 1967 I think. Surtees appeared, and I remember hiding the wing in the grass! But Robin Herd had written a couple of papers about wings; he was into wings. Bruce did several laps with it, and came in and said, "This is awful. It understeers everywhere around the racetrack. Take that thing off." And that's what we did. Pretty stupid. I don't know why it took us until 1969 to have a wing on the car.

I suppose the biggest step was that all-alloy engine that Reynolds did, where there were no liners in it. They developed the process of plating the pistons in conjunction with Chevrolet, for the Vega engine. How that came about, Bruce

Alexander

You used to run F1 and Can-Am cars at the same time; how did they compare from your technical point of view?

It tells you something that the F1 cars would break pieces from Can-Am cars. Hulme dropped out of the lead of a race at Spa while running a halfshaft off a Can-Am car. Whereas it lasted in Can-Am, it broke in F1.

The F1 cars were probably more advanced technically, and they were pretty agile, but that doesn't mean the Can-Am cars were crude, lumbering beasts. I tend to think of the 1969 car, the M8B, which was my favorite. Probably one of the best cars ever built. Fantastic race car, simple and quick and easy to work on. It had all the right things. Personally, I'd love to have all the drawings of that thing. If you built it nowadays using all the carbon fiber and modern, trick stuff, what a fantastic car you'd have.

And as usual, somebody panicked and the rules were screwed up for the next year.

The wing ban. Did McLaren experience any failure that would support the idea that mounting wings on the uprights was dangerous?

They did have one come off at Goodwood, early in testing of the M8B before they put those radius rods on. I don't recall any subsequent problem—although they did have a lot of cracks we had to keep chasing and welding up. I recall making new wing struts for every race. So they were stressed, but I don't remember any failure problems.

Seems to me the only thing that we had break that year was a bottom rear wishbone at Riverside on Bruce's car. It was a pretty good shunt.

When we had to take the wing off the uprights, it was a real pain in the ass. You had to have these unbelievable spring rates. Bruce schemed up a hydraulic device that adjusted the ride height. It was a big funny thing, sat on top of the gearbox and there was a couple of hydraulic cylinders underneath the springs. It was driven off the center of the rear antiroll bar, so roll wasn't affected by it. Any time that the car was pushed down by the aerodynamic load, this thing transferred fluid to the cylinders underneath the springs and raised the ride height back up.

Active suspension!

Yeah, it was a mechanical active suspension,

Still a band of bright, buoyant people, the Kiwis stood tall in the Can-Am through 1972. At Riverside that last year, Tyler appreciates a joke with Bruce's widow, Patty McLaren. *Dale von Trebra*

Crew Chief's Portfolio: Every so often Tyler stepped back from making history to record it. *Tyler Alexander*

in effect. I don't know if it ever worked. It didn't work the first time, then it sort of lingered around the workshop for ages. We never raced it. It was just one of the things that was tested.

You gotta remember, in those days we were doing things that were really nuts. We were racing Can-Am cars, Indy cars, Formula Two cars, Formula One cars, built a hillclimb car for somebody; I mean, we were doing unbelievable things with a very small number of people. The stuff wasn't particularly sophisticated, and maybe that's why we didn't do perhaps as well as we should have. Although, we were doing it. We were going to the races and we were doing reasonably well.

Why was McLaren so dominant in the Can-Am for so long?

We were more serious about it, and we worked harder. There were other people who tried. Lola was in there all the time. Chaparral had a pretty good stab at it. Ferrari made an attempt. But we had the luxury of being able to do a couple thousand miles of testing before the first race. I don't know why the others didn't.

Penske did. Penske was ready. I mean, even before the Porsche deal, when they were racing our old car against us, they were racing in the USRRC all summer leading up to the Can-Am in the fall, and racing is almost better than testing.

But even though they spent a lot of money and changed some stuff on it, it was still an older car. When I delivered [Bruce's championship-winning 1967 McLaren M6A] to Donohue, he said, "My God, this is the car that won all those races. What are you guys going to do now?" I said, "Well, actually I've got to get going because the plane leaves in about an hour and we're going home to build a better one." He just stood there with his mouth open. He even mentions that in his book [*The Unfair Advantage*, written with Paul Van Valkenburgh].

Also, you've got to remember—I don't know if I want to be rude about it—Bruce and Denny were real race drivers. I'm not sure that the other guys were. That, I'm sure, is why we won a lot of the races.

It was pretty tough against Surtees and some of those other guys. I think Surtees at some stages was better than us—whether his car was better or he was, I don't know. Hall was pretty good. Certainly Donohue was no slouch. And Gurney put a huge effort into his thing. Stewart was tough when he came in later on, for sure. He was the only one who could push the commitment to make his team work a lot harder. OK, there were a lot of good guys there, but, you know, they weren't racing in Europe all the time.

And those people came and went. We never let up. I don't think we ever took it for granted we were going to be quicker—although I remember the scene at Bridgehampton [1969], where we didn't practice on the second afternoon. But we never said, "We don't have to bother, because those guys aren't going to beat us anyway." We worked like hell for every single race. That part I distinctly remember.

Good and bad, how does the Can-Am stand in your mind?

For me, the bad part was that there was an enormous amount of work that nobody actually saw or thought we did. We worked all night before every Can-Am race. I must have done more all-nighters in the Can-Am series than I've ever done in my life. Probably because really we didn't have enough people. That's the only thing that comes to mind as the worst part.

The good part was the competition. In reality, I think it was good. Most of the atmosphere was good. The whole way the thing worked was very good. I remember the part about the parties and the girls. It was a good time in everybody's life.

It fits into the old deal with Harry Schell, or somebody: "What do you think of the racetrack?" He says, "Well, if we win it, we'll recommend it to everyone." So we won lots of races in the Can-Am series, and we're recommending it to everybody.

When did you ever get time to do all that fine photography?

I used to pinch the odd moment, grab the camera and wander around shooting pictures. Mostly in testing, not so much at the races. No one said, "You shouldn't be doing that, you ought to be working." One has the feeling someone would say that, now. Things are a lot more complicated.

1969: Bruce, Denny, Bruce, Denny . . .

McLaren's Greatest Season

This fourth year was the longest, and in some ways—certainly for some teams—the biggest. The number of races nearly doubled, to 11, while boosts in funding made the series the Million-Dollar Can-Am.

McLaren won every single race. No season better illustrates the old "Bruce and Denny Show" Can-Am catch-phrase, or more clearly illuminates why the Kiwis were so dominant. Primarily, they won because they focused on what it took to win. While the Can-Am was rightly known as the haven of innovation (ironically, that would never again be quite so true after this year), Bruce McLaren always approached new technology with cautious enthusiasm. After fielding distinctly new cars for each of the first three years, he and his tight-knit team were content to tackle 1969 with a mere revision of their 1968 model. And the McLaren M8B's most distinctive feature, its high, hub-mounted rear wing, was such an old idea that its inventor, Chaparral's Jim Hall, had now abandoned it.

Inside, though, the M8B had something uncommon in the Can-Am: development. Thoroughly tested, proven, and understood, it was more than fast enough, its handling was well balanced, and it was reliable. That last factor was the big key. McLaren had solved its big block Chevy problems of the year before, and out of the 24 race starts made by M8Bs in 1969 (in two events the factory ran three cars), there were just two engine breakdowns, and only four retirements in all.

To be sure, one of those was scary—Bruce's high-speed Riverside accident,

McLaren mastery: In 1969 the Can-Am grew from 6 to 11 rounds. Some expected a longer season would give other teams a better chance against the McLaren factory, which had won 9 races of the past 12. So how much tougher was it for the Bruce and Denny Show? As here at St. Jovite, they romped away with all 11 races. *Pete Biro*

Peeled orange: For 1969 McLaren finally adopted Chaparral's suspension-mounted rear wing to nail down the rear tires, but without the driver-trimmable feature. The M8B driver still had a clutch pedal to operate, so McLaren characteristically chose the most simple solution and fixed the wing's angle of incidence in the pits. That did cause more drag on straights, but the car's overall performance was good enough to win, and win, and win. *Pete Biro*

caused by rear suspension breakage. He got out of that one without injury (though a corner worker was hurt), and its main consequence was to show that Bruce and Denny's lighthearted-looking Show was really tough, exacting, dangerous work.

However, either McLaren or Hulme started from every pole that season, and they set fastest race lap 10 times. It was Bruce's turn to win the championship, and he did, earning 165 points to Denny's 160. The third-place driver, Chuck Parsons (Lola), scored but 81.

However, despite the look of the bare record, the cars coming to be known as the Orange Elephants were far from the only beasts in the Can-Am circus. A Prancing Horse was their strongest opposition. Driven by former McLaren man Chris Amon, this new version of 1968's ill-fated Ferrari 612P qualified third fastest four times, set fastest

Bruce at speed: For the first time since 1966, McLaren came to the Can-Am without an all-new car. The 1969 M8B was mainly a refurbished M8A from the previous season with aero refinements, including a high wing, plus a new, high-revving 430-ci Chevrolet engine. It was a relatively conservative approach, but that always worked for McLaren. By the time Bruce won Round 6, here at Elkhart Lake, he was on his way to his second championship. *Pete Biro*

race lap at Mid-Ohio, and briefly squeezed into the lead and finished second at Edmonton. But Amon's was a small team working far afield from an indifferent factory, and the only two engines it had often failed. Once, at Laguna Seca, Chris was so annoyed at the Ferrari that he guest-drove McLaren's third M8B.

A Road Runner—Chaparral—was another challenger. Not the radical 2H, which must go down in history as the only unsuccessful Chaparral model, but a McLaren M12 production car provided to John Surtees when the 2H wasn't ready. The 1966 series champion ran the white M12 in four races, was a second-row qualifier all four times, and repeatedly thrust himself into the lead at both Mosport and St. Jovite. Unfortunately, the thrusting led to shunting Bruce McLaren at the latter track, and in any case the Chaparral's Chevy engine never achieved reliability.

Teamwork: Though the driver gets most of the glory, racing really is a team sport. Bruce McLaren's winning personality attracted the best personnel in the game. *Pete Biro*

Can-Am drivers meet at Watkins Glen in 1969: (foreground) Denny Hulme; (sitting behind, from left) Unknown, Bruce McLaren, Jo Siffert, Chuck Parsons; (standing, from left) George Alderman, John Cordts, Oscar Koveleski, Leonard Janke; (background), John Surtees, Pedro Rodriguez. *Ray Jeanotte*

Others who put their faces in the McLaren mirrors that year, if only occasionally, included: Chuck Parsons in a hard-driven Lola T163-Chevy, who would finish third on points; Jo Siffert with a reliable Porsche 917PA "Porsche+Audi," eventual fourth in the standings; Dan Gurney, who usually drove his own modified McLaren M6B (a.k.a. the McLeagle), but who once took the spare factory M8B to a close third place; Jackie Oliver in the Bryant-built Ti22 "Titanium Car," which came in late but showed encouraging speed; and Mario Andretti, who beat Bruce in qualifying to start on the front row at Texas International Speedway, then headed Denny for four glorious, tire-blistering laps with an 8.1-liter Ford-engined M6B.

Andretti's demonstration of this powerhouse's potential was a hint of the kind of show the Can-Am could have become, but in the absence of serious commitment by Ford, Ferrari, or anyone else, it was Bruce and Denny (and Chevrolet) all the way.

Bruce McLaren (1969 McLaren M8B) founded the team that won more Can-Am races than any other. *Pete Biro*

Denny Hulme (at Laguna Seca) drove the well-balanced, highly-reliable, very fast M8B to total elimination in the 1969 series. *Pete Biro*

Cavallino Volante: Strongest challenge to McLaren's domination in 1969 came from former McLaren driver Chris Amon, who talked Ferrari into letting him campaign a revised prototype that briefly appeared late in 1968. The 612P, named for its 6.2-liter V-12, had enough power to keep McLaren's eyes on it, as here in Elkhart Lake's Thunder Valley. *Pete Lyons*

Uphill struggle: Unfortunately, Ferrari's tiny operation—one car, two engines, three people—couldn't compete with McLaren's depth. Usually, as here at Elkhart's Turn 5, Chris Amon battled to keep the M8Bs in sight. Once, when his last V-12 broke before a race, he guest-drove his old team's spare B-car. *Pete Lyons*

Boost on the bench: All through 1969 Amon's Ferrari mechanic Roger Bailey (later known as "Boost" for his work on McLaren's Indy Offies) devoted his English bulldog fighting spirit to keeping the single Italian car's only two engines alive thousands of miles from home. Co-crewman Doan "Studly" Spencer, at far right, pitches in late one night at Edmonton. *Pete Lyons*

Boost to come: Porsche's first foray into the Can-Am was normally aspirated, but Jo Siffert had a lead foot—demonstrated here at Riverside's Turn 8 at the top of the long straight—and the 917PA Spyder was almost fast enough. Though the cut-down enduro car was heavy, twitchy, and complex, it was very reliable. Despite missing three rounds of the series, Seppi only suffered two DNFs in his eight starts and came fourth in season points. *Pete Lyons*

Flightless bird: While admirable for the bold thinking it represented, Chaparral's 1969 Type 2H went down in history as Jim Hall's only significant failure. The idea was to maximize straightaway speed with a slim, low-profile coupe body. However, Hall was out of action following his 1968 accident, and the former Can-Am champion he hired, John Surtees, refused to race the car unless he could sit up to see out. Even then the man known as Fearless John called the short-wheelbase, narrow-track, de Dion–rear axle car "scary," and tacking on a huge wing (as shown during early practice at Riverside) didn't change his mind. *Pete Lyons*

Few people know that filmmaker George Lucas was a mega racing fan. The first draft of *Star Wars* had a Can-Am setting, and R2D2 originally was cast as a fireman at Mid-Ohio. His big scene would have involved a ride under the ultralow roof of the Chaparral 2H "quasi coupe." *Pete Lyons*

Chuck the Comet: One of the Can-Am's hardest working drivers was former United States Road Racing Champ Chuck Parsons, who led Lola's very small official factory effort to third place in the points this year. Here at Bridgehampton, he soldiered on with the T163 until his pit signaled that a replacement nosepiece was ready. *Pete Lyons*

Man on a mission: While active drivers like Bruce McLaren had to concentrate on their media relations, the retired Stirling Moss was free for more important pursuits. *Pete Lyons*

Boss at work: Even when he gave his body a break, Bruce McLaren's mind was always busy. As fine an engineer as he was a driver, but perhaps at his best as inspiration to his teammates, the New Zealander built a hot-rodded, third-hand Cooper (Roger Penske's former Zerex Special) into a major motorsports enterprise. Sadly, as he took this moment at Edmonton in July 1969, he had less than a year to live. *Pete Lyons*

McKees Mark 7. Turbocharger exhaust flames, a sight that would become familiar in road racing over the next decade, first appeared in the Can-Am this year. A twin-turbo installation on an iron-block, 389-ci Oldsmobile prepared by Gene Crowe, it was in the back of a McKee Mark 7 fitted with a unique "racer's wedge" body. Indy 500 star Joe Leonard drove it to eighth place in its debut at St. Jovite (shown here). A few weeks later at Elkhart Lake, Leonard tried out a mighty 455-inch turbo Olds in an entirely different McKee with four-wheel drive, an automatic transmission, and a flip-up air brake atop the engine. Unfortunately, the stimulatingly ambitious four-wheel-drive McKee Mark 14 never raced. *Pete Lyons*

Mann Open Sports Ford. Two years after the infamous *Honker II* so badly frightened Mario Andretti, Ford had the same English builder, Alan Mann Racing, produce a vehicle of similar design for the big block Ford engine. This package was better behaved, but the project ran even later than the earlier one, appearing only in time for the last two rounds of the 1969 season. Suspension failure dropped Frank Gardner out of seventh place at Riverside (where the shapely OSF is shown in the garage area), but at Texas World Speedway it lasted the distance to carry fellow Aussie Jack Brabham into third. Too bad Ford never took the Can-Am seriously. *Pete Lyons*

Core of the Kiwi brain trust was Bruce McLaren himself (in M8B cockpit, sheltering from sudden rain at Edmonton 1969), Tyler Alexander (far left), Denny Hulme (behind wing), and business partner and manager Teddy Mayer (right). *Pete Lyons*

Teddy Mayer

WHILE THE SHAPE of North America's Can-Am was strongly influenced by a New Zealander working in England, Bruce McLaren Motor Racing was shaped in great part by Americans. One in particular was McLaren's early investment partner, Edward Everett "Teddy" Mayer. While Brucie and his boys were out there gassing the mighty Orange Elephants to all those victories and championships, on the other side of the pit wall was Mayer, a.k.a. "the Wiener," his multitalented hands firmly on the financial, managerial, organizational, and legislative controls.

Though he originally intended to be a lawyer, Teddy turned out to be a deep-dyed racer and never got around to leaving the speed business. Perhaps ironically—but also probably inevitably—he now is with Roger Penske Racing, the organization whose Porsche Panzers pushed McLaren out of the Can-Am.

I don't really think back on the Can-Am very often. The interest is in what we're doing now and in the future. But I definitely enjoyed it. We learned a hell of a lot in a very short period of time, which to me is the interesting part of any series. The change in technology over that nine-year span was absolutely fantastic. Now, we're getting finer and finer detail of improvement, but over longer and longer periods.

The Can-Am days were fun, but the technology has moved on. You really are in a different era totally in terms of the engineering and science and knowledge that you can apply to the problem. I feel like that was stone-age.

I remember one time when we were testing at Goodwood, and we cut a hole in the top of the nose behind the radiator. Bruce tried it and said, "No, no, that makes it oversteer a lot. That's no good." What we were totally missing was that it oversteered, yeah, because we'd taken a lot of lift out of the front end. We needed to put a ton of rear wing on to balance it, but in those days we didn't really think about it very well. We weren't aerodynamically savvy.

Nowadays, at Penske, we spend three weeks in a wind tunnel doing 14 hours in a day. We do six or seven thousand runs in a year. There are four guys in the model department, plus two draftsmen and the designer, and that's all they do full time. In the beginning at McLaren, that many people was our whole team.

Can-Am cars were certainly the highest-powered road race cars in those days, by a long way. They didn't handle badly, either. We were maybe ahead of the tires; we can only go as fast as our tire technology will allow. But our lap times in the Can-Am cars usually were quicker in those days than they were in the Formula Ones, so they were the premiere road racing cars of the time.

Can you put into words why the McLaren team was so successful?

Well, we had a bunch of very pragmatic people, including Bruce, who focused on the problems and came up with solutions. They all worked very hard. It always takes hard work to be successful.

One year Gordon Coppuck designed a spun magnesium wheel center. We had a slightly different engine. Somebody came up with a different oil tank package, and there was some other problem, I can't remember what it was. Anyway, we went down to Goodwood to do our final test. It was total disaster. The wheels ran a lap or half a lap before they broke. The oil tank flung oil all over the place. And whatever our other problems were, they were pretty bad as well. So we went back to the shop, and we worked from Monday night until Friday morning nonstop. Put the cars on the airplane and won 11 out of 11 races. So even in those days, there was plenty of work.

By 1972, McLaren's state-of-the-art headquarters in England was bursting with activity on many racing fronts. Working with mechanics to complete a brand new Chevy-powered M20 Can-Am car is designer Gordon Coppuck (facing camera). The M16 Indy machine with its Drake-Offy turbo engine (No. 12) is a few feet away. In the background both a Cosworth Chevy Vega-powered M21 F2 and a Cosworth Ford-engined M19 "YardleyMac" F1 can be seen. *Pete Lyons*

That was so impressive, how at the end of a race everybody else in the paddock would be opening beer and trading war stories, and over in the corner there's the McLaren team cleaning and studying things and already thinking about the next race.

Yeah. The good teams do the same thing today. You have data available at the end of the race that isn't available at any other time. You really need to collect it, whether you're doing it with a computer or eyeball.

You're only as good as your last race.

Was that you who created that work ethic in the team?

Oh, no. Bruce was a hard worker as well. And Tyler [Alexander, crew chief] has always been the hardest on himself and the crew. It's impossible to say too much about Tyler. He's just a real workhorse that got on with his job, kept his eye on the ball, and solved the problems as they came along.

It's funny, but although we worked hard, we had more time to talk to other teams and socialize and have a good time than by rights you have nowadays. Cars are a lot more complicated now. There's so much technology, and so much data to analyze, so many bases to cover, so much to do.

In the Can-Am days, we had a crew of two mechanics for each car. Now you have three mechanics, a fabricator, a tire guy, an electronics engineer, a race engineer, an engine guy—on each car. Yet they have less time to themselves than our mechanics had in those days.

Were you surprised that year after year nobody came forth to mount an effective challenge?

A little bit. Lola had the resources, certainly. So did March, and Ferrari made an effort. A number of people had the resources, but they were by and large not very successful at it until Porsche came along. They hadn't done their homework, I guess. You don't show up at the first race unprepared if you want to win.

Like Denny said, "We come prepared to race. The other guys come prepared to test."

That's exactly right. But why they did that, I don't know.

Talk about the drivers.

Bruce was a wonderful person. Very patient, very honest, a good engineer, and not a bad driver at all. I'd say his one fault was that if he had a theory as an engineer, he'd tend to be a little too favorable about that theory as a

McLaren also maintained an engine shop in Detroit, where Lee Muir (foreground in picture taken during 1970) conjured power from giant lumps of Reynolds aluminum. *Pete Lyons*

driver. Several times, I think, we got slightly led astray in some of Bruce's favorite theories, mainly because he'd thought them up and he wanted them to work!

Denny Hulme actually was more critical and less biased than Bruce as a test driver. Denny was a very good Can-Am driver. That kind of car liked to be driven quite smoothly, and Denny was very smooth, always. He got a lot out of the car, but he was easy on the equipment. He finished a lot of races, as opposed to, oh, maybe the likes of Jackie Stewart.

Jackie was definitely faster than Denny in F1, but in a Can-Am car maybe not necessarily any faster. I think Jackie tried to drive it like an F1 car, which was a more nimble, lighter car with more tire per pound, and it required a more aggressive driving style. Not to say that Jackie wasn't very good, but I think Denny was better in a Can-Am car than Jackie was.

Ever mindful of the most minute detail, Mayer (a.k.a. "the Wiener") checks the St. Jovite scales against a known quantity before the race car is rolled across. Hulme and Gurney are more interested in the 1970 M8D itself. *Pete Lyons*

Stewart was going to join you for 1972, but came down with an ulcer.

Jackie always operated on a fairly high stress base, he imposed a lot on himself. He drove at 100 percent all the time, and then he was more involved in PR and promoting the team and himself than Denny ever was. That takes a lot of time and a lot of energy. It puts a lot of stress on you.

Drivers now do a huge amount more of that stuff than they did in those days. Our guys here at Penske hardly have a spare moment. They're at some kind of a function, if they're not driving, every day, all day.

How do they stand that?

They bitch and moan. We have to have a PR person with each one of them at all times, to be sure they attend the function and they're on time, and know who they're meeting, what the idea is. I mean, they do a good job. They're all very professional. But it's hard work. They're exhausted at the end of the weekend.

It sure was different in the old Can-Am. I'm thinking of how often we used to see Denny taking a nap! How about Dan Gurney?

Dan was good, but I really couldn't compare him with Bruce or Denny, because he didn't have enough time to get totally adjusted before the oil company sponsorship conflict came into play.

Was that amicable, by the way?

Yeah, very. His oil company said, hey, wait a minute. We don't really want the other oil company advertising on his car. Gulf said, well, in that case, we really don't want to have him driving. But there wasn't any screaming match or anything. We just made some other arrangements.

Peter Revson was a very good Can-Am driver. I think actually he was best at driving Indy Cars. He was extraordinary in them, but he didn't like driving them. I think he thought it was more dangerous. We often had to force him to; we had disagreements in that area. After Indy Cars, he was probably equally good in F1 and a Can-Am car. But he was improving as a driver all the time. He was definitely becoming a great driver.

Revvie liked driving Can-Am cars. He enjoyed the circuit; he had a good time doing it. Big-time motor racing was almost brand new in the United States. There was Indy, but the USAC Trail was pretty small-time stuff, whereas the Can-Am attracted a lot of glamour. The excitement and the newness of it, the feeling of it growing and developing; everybody enjoyed that.

One of the better stories: I remember a Can-Am race at Riverside where Pete Revson hadn't done very well. I just sort of made a slightly disparaging remark about his performance, which I thought was subpar. The next morning we decided we were going to test. Pete had a hangover. He invited me to ride with him and see what the thing was doing, which I foolishly did. He actually ran a lap that was faster than his fastest race lap. Scared the shit out me! It was revenge, I suppose.

No "suppose" about it! And what about the McLaren cars; do you think you reached the optimum design for the Can-Am in that period? Or looking back, would you have done something different?

It would have been difficult to do much different. You couldn't spend as much time testing as we do now. We didn't have separate test teams, like we have now, with 12 and 15 people in them to send off on their own projects. And we had to work with gearboxes that were available, as opposed to designing custom gearboxes as we do now as a matter of course. So you had to move rather carefully. Within the constraints of the budget, we built a pretty good race car.

We always kept our cars pretty light and simple. Bruce did resist going to the big block engines for a while, and he was quite right in saying that a light, nimble car is a better package than a big, heavy one. But in those days we didn't have computers to analyze how much time we spend in the straights and how much in the corners, and feed in some changes, and say okay, this is the optimum setup, this is the optimum gear ratio, this is the optimum engine for the tires we have, and decide what the best compromise is for all the circuits we run on. We couldn't even begin to do anything like that. Now, we do that as a matter of course before we decide anything.

In the end, the Reynolds aluminum Chevy blocks were a lot bigger engines and a lot more powerful and not that much heavier than the Oldsmobiles we started out with. There were some iron block

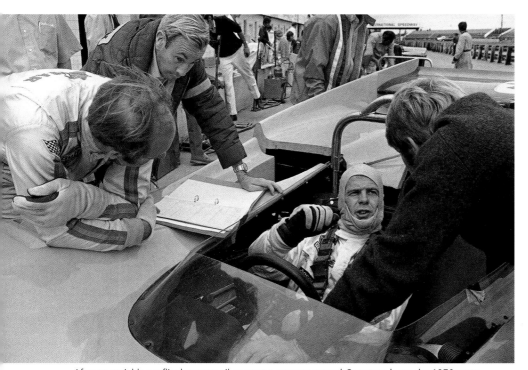

After an amiable conflict between oil company sponsors caused Gurney to leave the 1970 team, McLaren turned to British F5000 champion Peter Gethin. Here at his first Can-Am, Edmonton, Gethin tells Hulme (left), Mayer, and Alexander what he thinks of the big Batmobile. Presumably, he's not saying anything about winning Elkhart Lake later on. *Pete Lyons*

ones in between that weren't ideal. But when we got to the really good Chevy aluminum blocks, we had a pretty good package overall.

Why did Bruce turn to North American sports car racing? Was that your influence as an American?

No, it was a step between what he'd been doing and F1. The Can-Am was the next most lucrative and professional series around after F1, but F1 was hard to get into. We thought we should do this first. Bruce had done some racing over here [United States] and liked it. We were able to raise some money to do it. We had some equipment that was suitable, the Zerex Special car and the aluminum Oldsmobile engine, so we went from there. Obviously, the success was good publicity for us.

Did the Can-Am end up being more lucrative than F1? I remember the Europeans being all agog at how much money there was available in the Can-Am.

It was more lucrative in terms of prize money. Because we had a lot of success, obviously we took the lion's share of that. That helped. Really, the top one or two teams in F1 were probably doing a lot better than we were in those days, but the other teams, probably not.

We didn't really totally separate out our Formula One and our Can-Am finances from each other. There wasn't much point, it was all one company. I think we were spending roughly the same in F1 and Can-Am in say 1967–68, but we were concentrating on the Can-Am.

Denny said, "Everybody thought we earned so much money, but we were really on a shoestring. At Edmonton on Monday morning we were down there with our gold bars turning them into cash so we could pay our motel bill."

Well, that's a little apocryphal. We were always able to pay the bills, we were able to operate reasonably. But we needed all the money. Our total income might have been half a million for our best Can-Am season. Our budget was probably in the three or four hundred thousand dollars bracket. We weren't all putting a huge amount of money in our banks.

Remember, depending on the driver and his contract, he would get anywhere from 30 to 50 percent of the prize money. The crew would get probably 10 or 15. So you'd be looking at 40 to 50 percent to the team budget. We needed that money as well. As I say, we weren't desperate to pay our hotel bills, but you needed it all in the end to add up to a balance or a small profit.

I've been told by a lot of Monday morning quarterbacks [outsiders] that, if we'd kept one model of every car we ever made, we'd be billionaires. Yeah, but we needed to sell the cars at the end of the season to go forward.

Now that you're with Roger, has he told you how much the Porsche budget was in 1972?

You know, I've never really discussed it with him.

Just what was your relationship with Chevrolet? I'm remembering the laugh Bruce got when he accepted his championship trophy in 1969, and he said, "I'd like to thank Chevrolet, but they wouldn't know what I was talking about." However, those bow-ties must have been on the cars for a reason. Did their sizes from year to year indicate the degree of support?

Initially, Chevrolet helped us with a little advice on engineering and technology. Then they started supplying things like heads and other equipment to us, and eventually some financial support as well.

They were very helpful, but in those days they didn't want to advertise it too blatantly, so I wouldn't say the relative sizes of their logos were in the right proportion to their involvement. But in the end, the support from Chevrolet and from Goodyear was probably about equal to that from Gulf.

After Bruce's accident in 1970, how did the team keep going?

Well, it was fairly simple. It was either stop everything or try to carry on. It seemed like Bruce would have wanted us to carry on. In those days, death in motor racing was a lot more common than it is now. F1 killed probably a couple people a year on average. So we were accustomed—not happy about, believe me, or frightened by it—but accustomed to that happening. You had a simple choice: either stop, or carry on and try to build better, safer cars and race them. We chose to go forward.

Denny was a tower of strength at that time.

Well, he was. Remember that he'd just burned his hands at Indy. They were quite painful. Yeah, he was a very level head. He drove well considering the pain he was in. He was a morale booster, definitely.

And Dan was very good. He was the right man at the right time. Dan is enthusiastic and charming and energetic and gets people working for him and with him. People are always going to rally around the drivers, since the drivers are encouraging to the people.

Though he set out to be a lawyer and wound up running the business side of McLaren, Mayer has always been fascinated by the technology of racing. At Riverside 1969, he took a moment from management to help clean an M8B's Hewland gearbox. Note how the wing struts mount directly on the wheel hub uprights, sending downforce directly to the tires. Unlike the old Chaparrals, this McLaren kept its wing at one angle. *Pete Lyons*

I think Phil Kerr at that stage was very helpful. He had a steady hand on things back at base, and that helped a lot.

All the guys on the team obviously pulled together. They all did a good job, all the mechanics and engine builders and so on. Those are the guys who really motivated the team, I'd say.

At the end of the 1970 season, when the controversy peaked about the Chaparral 2J ground effects car, or the Sucker, you were adamantly against it. You were actually bitter; I remember you telling me that you felt the previous year's ban on high-mounted wings killed your partner, so this sort of end-run on the ban wasn't fair.

Well, I was bitter about the Sucker. For one thing, I thought it was an unnecessary escalation of the costs. More important, I thought it was very dangerous. Whenever the car went, not even off the road but over something on the track, there would be a small showering of the people behind with all sorts of nasty things from the fans. I don't think that's terribly clever or very safe.

And I think the fans themselves were inherently not fail-safe [i.e., if something in the system failed, the car became more difficult to control—Author] Part of myself, if you like, ever since my younger brother, Tim, was killed, is that I'm always trying to keep an eye on the rules and everything else to make racing as safe as possible. It's not a safe sport as we all know. But you can do things to make it worse, or you can do things to make it better. I really feel the Sucker was counterproductive in terms of safety.

When I said the wing ban led to Bruce's death, okay, it was a mechanical failure or whatever you want to call it. The body catches came out, and the whole rear section fell off. We were using stick pins, and under certain conditions of vibration they will fail, they will shake out. We suspect that's what happened. We found the pin somewhere down the track, so it was put in. But whether it was put in properly or improperly you'll never know.

However, if the rear wing had been mounted directly on the suspension uprights, as in 1969, when the tail came off you presumably wouldn't have had the huge change in the center of aerodynamic pressure that put him out of control.

I still feel there's nothing wrong with a wing mounted on the uprights. That actually is a very good aerodynamic package. You don't get pitch change from the added aerodynamics. It makes the car much easier to balance. I think that they were banning the wrong thing.

What should they have banned?

Bad engineering, which should always be banned. It's difficult to police, I understand. But it is what gets most people.

The trouble with wings in those days was that we didn't really know the forces that we were generating, and we didn't do careful analysis of the structures needed to mount them. However, at McLaren we never had a catastrophic failure, except the one that killed Bruce in 1970, and that wasn't a wing failure.

What went into your decision to pull out of the Can-Am after 1972?

It was strictly an economic and logistic decision. We did build a turbo engine, as you know. We got to the point of running it on the racetrack. I think the thing would have been more than competitive on horsepower with the Porsche. We saw around 1,200 horsepower, I believe.

But obviously it needed a new transmission, new axles, and a whole new running gear, and it all would have needed a lot of development, a lot of testing. We didn't really have either the time or the money at that stage.

Did you lobby to have turbos banned?

I suppose we did.

What was the SCCA response?

I can't remember specifically, but I guess they would have said it was within the rules. Apart from, in the end, having no aerodynamic devices on the uprights and a few things like that, it was a wide-open series.

Do you think the original Formula Libre concept of the Can-Am was inherently viable, or did it contain inherent flaws?

I think it contained inherent flaws, like any wide-open situation. When you get someone with more money or engineering available to them, they will eventually dominate. If there's no

Amidst the epics of work, there were snapshots of fun. *Tyler Alexander*

limitation, you can go berserk, just do whatever you want. It's what you see in Formula One right now with the domination of one or two teams. Their rules are far less tightly drawn than CART rules, and provided you have the money and expertise, it's easier to get a significant advantage.

Looking at the future, do you see any way that big league sports car racing could be resurrected?

No, I don't think so, to be honest. Single seater racing seems to have taken over as the dominant factor. There's only normally room for one super-expensive formula. I don't see sports car racing coming back.

You said the Can-Am attracted a lot of glamour. I've heard stories from some of the guys about what was going on after a race that I didn't know about, because I was off in my van typing my story that night.

Yeah, definitely. Quite a lot.

Let the record show you're laughing. I got into the wrong end of it, I think!

Could well be!

1970: A New Era

Can-Am Goes Conventional

With the new decade came a new-look Can-Am. Up until now, providing there was enough cockpit space for two seats and each wheel remained covered by fenders, the cars had been practically unlimited. But for 1970, the Canadian and U.S. series administrators buckled under European (FIA) pressure to ban so-called "moving aerodynamic devices."

This outlawed any of the driver-operated "flippers" and/or wheel-hub-mounted airfoils pioneered by Chaparral in 1965–1966 and adopted by others through 1969. Additional minor bodywork regulations, such as requiring windscreens to be symmetrical left-and-right and mandating tail-end panels to keep rear tires from spitting stones (not itself a bad idea), forced the cars into a more conventional mold. As a side effect of the new rules, tall engine intake airscoops were forbidden. Thus, a stroke of the international pen clamped North America's wild-and-free Can-Am beast into its first chains. Or so most people expected. A few innovative minds still found some aerodynamic tricks to pull.

First, though, the Can-Am community had to deal with the tragic loss of Bruce McLaren in a testing accident in England just 12 days before the first race of the season. Universally liked and admired, the smiling New Zealander had done such a good job so graciously that nobody really begrudged the way he seized the Can-Am and made it his own. Another blow was the fatal crash of McLaren M6B owner-driver

The Bear vs. The Sucker: By the end of the year, McLaren's lead driver was up to speed but so was the new Chaparral 2J Ground Effect Vehicle. Here at Riverside, Vic Elford out-qualified Hulme by a whopping 2.2 seconds. Off track Denny lobbied against the innovative machine, but once the racing started he just spoke with his foot. In the end, he won his second Can-Am title and the fourth in a row for Bruce McLaren Motor Racing. *John Rettie*

Big Dan: First Denny Hulme suffered badly burned hands at Indianapolis. Then Bruce McLaren was killed in a testing accident at Goodwood just days before the first Can-Am in 1970. His grieving teammates could have collapsed. Instead, they turned to sometime racing rival and eternal friend Dan Gurney to keep the McLaren winning streak going here at Mosport and St. Jovite. *Pete Lyons*

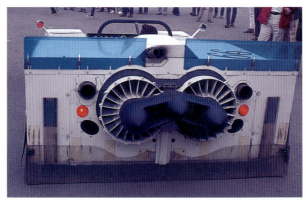

Fan car: The sensation of 1970 was Chaparral's 2J. Originally a test bed built by Chevrolet R&D, it made use of the ground effects principle to generate atmospheric downforce independent of vehicle speed. Although the complex vehicle was heavy and troublesome, its extra tire adhesion through slow turns usually made it the fastest car around the track. That included here at Laguna Seca, where Vic Elford qualified on pole—although he would miss the race due to failure of the main engine. The Chaparral's troubles didn't mollify rival manufacturers, who argued that its "moving aerodynamic devices" (skirts as well as fans) violated the new-for-1970 rule banning suspension-mounted and/or pivoting body parts. The controversy finally went to Paris, where the FIA declared the 2J illegal. Jim Hall, whose Chaparral innovations did so much to attract fans to the early Can-Am, lost interest and quit. *John Rettie*

Dick Brown at Mosport during practice the day before the opening race. These deaths, the first in the Can-Am series, took a lot of fun out of the game.

Bruce McLaren's team was further crippled by burns Denny Hulme had suffered to his hands at Indianapolis. No outsider would have blamed the Kiwis for skipping this race entirely. But they came. They qualified fastest. They won. It was Dan Gurney who stood in for Bruce, putting a brand-new McLaren M8D on pole and backing Hulme in the race until Denny's tender and bleeding hands gave out. Then Gurney ran down a remarkably quick Jackie Oliver in the "Titanium Car" and added one more victory to the McLaren account—the factory team's 14th straight. Gurney went on to win the second round, at St. Jovite, then a sponsorship conflict forced him to leave the team. His replacement was British Formula 5000 champion Peter Gethin, who later in the season was able to notch a Can-Am win of his own.

Denny Hulme was back up to speed by the third race. He won at Watkins Glen and went on to a total of six victories and his second Can-Am

Titanium Car: Though not as technically exciting as a Chaparral, the American-made Bryant Ti22 was a light, nimble race car capable of challenging McLaren drivers. At Mosport, Jackie Oliver (No. 22) held off Dan Gurney (No. 48 McLaren M8D "Batmobile") to lead many laps and finish second. Unfortunately, this team's promising challenge would be derailed by a first-lap flip at the next race. *Bill Oursler*

Lola: Once its curvaceous T70 was the very definition of a top Can-Am car, but by 1970 Lola had only one strong entry. The T220 had some good design points, and rising star Peter Revson drove it hard—hard enough to lead one race and qualify on pole for another. But most of the testing was conducted during the race season (here it heads into the Mosport pits with broken suspension), and this team was another that never matched McLaren. *Pete Lyons*

Champagne Peter: Revson was one of sports car racing's many rich kids, but he didn't let that handicap him. His dedication to the job earned him as much respect from his peers as his driving ability, which was outstanding. In 1970 he was already a member of McLaren's Indy team, and he would soon join the team for Can-Am and F1. *Pete Lyons*

March: Another car that might have won races if the team had started earlier, the March 707 was designed by former McLaren engineer Robin Herd, and driven by former McLaren driver Chris Amon. Lap times were good on its debut here at Donnybrooke, but that was Round 8 of a 10-race season, and there wasn't enough time left to get the 707 debugged. *Pete Lyons*

BRM: Attracted to the Can-Am by new rules that mandated more conventional cars, British F1 constructor BRM expanded its operations with this Chevy-powered two-seater called the P154. Like so many would-be McLaren beaters, the team was just barely ready for the first race. Here designer Tony Southgate, at left, paces his creation as bystanders help push it to life for its first-ever run late Friday evening at Mosport. Canadian George Eaton and Mexico's Pedro Rodriguez in a second car drove hard, but the BRM was hard to handle and hard to keep running. *Pete Lyons*

Shadow: Flying in the face of the trend toward cars that looked alike, Don Nichols' first Shadow used small wheels and "tiny" tires to lower the body line and thus increase straightaway speed. That part worked, but the rest of a very ambitious concept didn't. After George Follmer and Vic Elford (shown here in the second version at Mid-Ohio) struggled with handling, braking, and overheating problems through just three races, Shadow pulled the car out to try something a little more conventional. *Pete Lyons*

driver's championship. From the bare racing record (9 McLaren wins in 10 starts), it would be hard to tell anything was different for the bereaved Kiwis. That was despite relatively serious efforts from several manufacturers of "conventional" cars built to the new rules, plus a couple of decidedly unconventional end-runs.

The biggest threat on sheer lap speed was an all-new Chaparral with novel aerodynamics. Officially it was known as the type 2J Ground Effect Vehicle, but various people called it the Fan Car, Sucker, or Sweeper. The nicknames came from the pair of ducted extraction fans on the tail. Driven by an independent, two-cylinder engine, these fans created an atmospheric pressure differential inside the reinforced body. There were sliding plastic skirts between the body and the track surface to seal the pressure. This big, blunt box of a car was essentially a giant suction cup sticking itself to the road.

Here was one crazy Can-Am idea that worked. Everywhere it went, the Chaparral 2J proved fastest around the track. Jackie Stewart drove it to best race lap at Watkins Glen, then Vic Elford put it on pole for Road Atlanta, Laguna Seca, and Riverside. The car's cornering speed was a decisive advantage, particularly through the slow-to-medium speed turns characterizing most North American road courses. Rival teams protested. Led by McLaren's Teddy Mayer, they argued that the fans and

Pete Lyons

Finest feature: Aside from big power, the best thing about the old Can-Ams were their passenger seats—true sports cars.
Pete Lyons

Ford G7A. Another FoMoCo Can-Am effort that faded, this roadster was one of two built on unused aluminum honeycomb chassis of Ford's 1967 Mark IV Le Mans coupe. Originally these cars were nicknamed "Calliopes" for an intricate-looking big engine, and Mario Andretti was going to race them in 1968. When one car finally appeared in 1969, it was in the private hands of two brothers named Agapiou. During that season and the next, they entered it as the Ford G7A with several big Ford engines and with several drivers, but with little success. Here at Riverside 1970 it was John Cannon's turn. That day the car's career came to an end in a fiery crash. (Nobody was hurt.) *Bob Tronolone*

diameter brakes faded badly, the tiny tires bounced off every bump, and handling was visibly erratic. Overheating was a persistent problem, too, a direct consequence of compromises the new bodywork rules forced in the original design. Nichols pulled the radical vehicle out after only three brief appearances (by George Follmer and Vic Elford), but he would return with a series of ever more conventional Shadows, until success was finally achieved.

There was a third amazing machine in that year's series, although it didn't actually start a race. If two engines in the Chaparral seemed extreme, how about four? With its quartet of two-cylinder, two-stroke engines driving all four wheels, the *Mac's-It Special* was the kind of bold experiment that some people believed the Can-Am was all about.

skirts violated the new rule about "moving aerodynamic devices." Some drivers also complained the Sweeper was jetting track debris into their faces. Never mind that the 2J was a complex new machine that suffered from reliability problems. It only started three races all season (scratching from Laguna with a scattered engine), and only finished one. Ban it, demanded the protesters. The bitter controversy lasted past the end of the season and was finally decided by the FIA in Paris. When the ruling went against him, Jim Hall quit building his innovative Chaparrals, and the Can-Am lost one of its most exciting marques.

The second unusual car concept of 1970 was the *Tiny Tire* AVS Shadow. Advanced Vehicle Systems (AVS) was a company set up by racing entrepreneur Don Nichols to build a car that would win by going faster in a straight line—the opposite of Chaparral's faster-cornering approach. Firestone agreed to engineer special tires 7 inches smaller in diameter than normal, which allowed a much lower body line. The idea was that less frontal area meant less air-drag. The idea worked, but the car didn't. The Shadow was indeed a rocket on the straightaways, but its small-

More practical-minded racers knew the Can-Am was really about putting together a simple, reliable, adequately fast car in time to race it hard from round one—the McLaren strategy. Several teams made efforts to follow it this year. One strong contender was the "Titanium Car," the Ti22 designed by Peter Bryant and driven spiritedly by Jackie Oliver. Unfortunately, the middle portion of the season was lost when the car flipped over backward on the first lap of the second race, St. Jovite. There wasn't a replacement ready until Laguna Seca, round nine.

Lola, once dominant in Can-Am and good enough to place its driver, Chuck Parsons, third in 1969, came back with a new T220. Rising star—and future champion—Peter Revson took it to the front a couple of times and might have been a more consistent contender, had the factory started the season with a race car, rather than a prototype.

March, a new company, came into the fray at midseason with a new car called the 707. Driven by Chris Amon, formerly with McLaren and

Ferrari, it was fast when it held together. Again, more might have happened if it had happened sooner. The BRM P154 was another promising design handicapped by poor factory support.

Given enough depth in their teams, any of these "conventional cars" powered by conventional big block Chevy engines might have beaten the McLaren-Chevies. Instead, when the Kiwi winning streak was finally broken at 19, it was by a privateer Porsche driver with the smallest engine in the field: a 3.0-liter. His little 308 was an endurance racer, but Road Atlanta turned out to be an endurance race, and Tony Dean couldn't believe his luck.

Rattenbury Mark 4. Jim Rattenbury, a Canadian mechanical engineer, stepped up to the big class with this car in 1965. He used a Huffaker Genie Mark 8 body, some other Genie parts such as wheels and spindles, and some of a Genie space frame. He finished the frame himself, built his own suspension and fuel tanks, and solved the transaxle problem by turning a Chevy Corvair unit back-to-front. His engine was Oldsmobile's little "Aluminum 8," for which he fabricated his own carburetor manifold and ignition system. The declared weight that has come down through history is an impressively minimal 1,100 pounds. After crashing his Mark 4 in 1966, Rattenbury sold it to countryman Mike Barbour, who eventually entered it in a few 1970 Can-Ams (he's shown here at Elkhart Lake). By then the Rattenbury was a time machine, but it did qualify for three races, and finished two. *Pete Lyons*

Porsche 908. Although the Can-Am had no upper limit on engine size, there was a minimum of 2.5 liters. That permitted England's Tony Dean to run the series with his 3.0-liter Porsche endurance car. For two seasons, 1969 and 1970, he had a wonderful time throwing his nimble, reliable little car around North American tracks (shown here at Elkhart Lake 1970) and picking up lavish Can-Am prize monies. Those two seasons Dean wound up a respectable eighth and sixth in the championship, respectively, and finished races as high as fourth. But of course he had no hope of winning—until the fast guys all fell off the road at Road Atlanta 1970. That's how a Porsche broke McLaren's 19-race winning streak. *Pete Lyons*

Dan Gurney

On Bruce McLaren's death, Dan Gurney helped hold the team together by winning the first two Can-Ams of 1970. Here at Mosport he balances the new M8D against the mighty torque of a 465-inch Chevy. *Pete Lyons*

ONE OF AMERICA'S ALL-TIME OUTSTANDING DRIVERS, Big Dan won races both domestically and internationally in all sorts of race cars, from Indy cars to stock cars to sports cars to enduro cars to Formula One. After his retirement in 1970, having founded All American Racers to build Eagles, he continued to win as a constructor in USAC Indy Cars, IMSA GTO, and GTP.

Although other commitments as well as ongoing engine disappointments kept Gurney from giving the Can-Am the attention it required—and that he always hoped to give it—he did take three race victories during his five years of participation, and he still remembers the grand old series fondly.

The Can-Am was great motor racing, I thought. The big, push-rod American powerplants meant it was sort of the strong heartbeat of racing. And then it was off the edge of things technologically. We had tremendous advances in technology, especially in aerodynamics, in those years. There was a good deal of the unknown.

Gurney and McLaren respected each other as competitors, liked one another as friends, and valued the other as a team member—each raced the other's F1 cars at times. *Pete Lyons*

Dan won the second-ever Can-Am, at Bridgehampton 1966, in his Lola T70 powered by a small block Ford 305 equipped with his own Gurney-Weslake heads. This would remain the only Ford victory in the old series. *Pete Biro*

You never knew what else was going to happen, which was the fun of it.

It was something you did in the off-season, at least if you were already doing F1 and Indy cars, as we were. You could see that Bruce McLaren and Teddy Mayer and some of their connections got the drop on a lot of us, because they were more than competitive from the financial angle, which was pretty important.

You were pretty competitive with your Lola T70s with small block Fords. You won the second-ever Can-Am race, Bridgehampton 1966. You were on two poles that year, and got another pole as late as Riverside 1967.

I don't know. We were crossing our fingers all the time, just trying to keep things together. That time at Riverside, we had 374 inches. Pretty big for a small block Ford. Just one that we had bored out and stroked, and built with our Gurney-Weslake heads on it. It was good enough to be on pole, but it only lasted two laps in the race. Detonated itself to smithereens.

Weren't you responsible for the longer and lower noses that started appearing on the T70s?

Probably. It was for better stick. See, they had quite a bit of toboggan there, originally. Used to lift.

I'd say in its day the Lola was the best one out there, but all those cars were trying to find their way into aerodynamics. When you have that much bodywork, plus that much power and tire, you're going to become involved in aerodynamics. Most of us didn't know how to spell aerodynamics. We just knew that if we could get some, we could win races!

One of the finest of American drivers, a winner in many different forms of racing, Gurney also founded the great All American Racers Eagle car building operation. One of his early steps to that end was a highly modified McLaren M6B, which inevitably and immediately was dubbed the "McLeagle." *Pete Lyons*

Gurney's original idea for the McLeagle in 1968 was a compact, lightweight, low-drag special powered by a relatively small, high-winding Ford—a two-seat Grand Prix car. He persevered with that concept into 1969, as shown here at St. Jovite. *Pete Lyons*

By the end of 1969, Gurney was a convert to big block Chevy power and high-downforce aerodynamics. This is the McLeagle at Laguna Seca. *Bob Tronolone*

What was awfully interesting to me was that most of the good aerodynamicists in those days were aircraft guys, and they generally told you to have that toboggan-like shape on the lower edge of the nose, which of course was lifting the whole bloody setup. They'd look you right in the face and tell you that's the right way for it to be. I don't want to blanket the whole group, but most of them wouldn't admit that there was some difference in car aerodynamics versus aviation.

Gradually, they had to. It's the same damn air and the same damn laws, but different applications.

Then in 1968 you modified an M6B McLaren and called it a McLeagle.

We worked with that for two years, and managed to never, ever get it to where it should have been. It was like the front wasn't attached to the back, and vice-versa. Unpredictable. It was one of those things that, if you were really good, you could cope with it in the dry. But heaven help you if it became wet. Diabolical!

I tried to correct that by making sort of farmer-like changes, and found out that I could succeed in making it worse, but I couldn't seem to make it better. If you're just sort of eyeballing things and say, "Let's put the hinge point here, or change the angle of the this and the that," it's amazing how easy it is to never hit it. But that's what we were doing.

We could have gone back to the way it had been, but it wasn't that good to start with. I tried to generate knowledge by asking quote experts unquote, and we changed the suspension geometry more than once. More than twice. I think we took some weight off, and I think we actually improved it from the aero aspect. But that's only one part of the equation. We never did get that fundamental, mechanical chassis part of it right.

So that's what the McLeagle was, just one of those unfinished symphony deals. It was a fun name, anyway.

At the Michigan race in 1969, you stepped from your own McLeagle into the third factory McLaren, an M8B. Was that car in any way a revelation in terms of technology or power or anything like that?

Uhm, it was what I expected power-wise. But aerodynamically it had a larger sweet spot, and the brakes were very good. Also the shock absorbers and the suspension travel were much better, and it could cope with more irregularities without being upset.

At that track, on the road course, you had to cross the speedway section, and it was pretty rough. Our car would just about break in half going across there. These things would kind of soak it up. It was like a night and day difference.

Hell, it was damn easy to do very well with that car, like taking candy from a baby. Which is what the technology is supposed to enable you to do. It was a competent machine.

"Aerodynamic sweet spot?"

Well, if you're accelerating off a corner and the nose lifts and the thing goes into a big understeer, or you do the opposite under braking and it goes into an oversteer condition, then it probably has a smaller sweet spot. Or if it does one thing with the tanks full, and something else when it's light. The M8B had, for its day, a very large sweet spot.

I finished third there.

Behind McLaren and Hulme in the other two McLarens, starting from the back of the grid. I've always been sure you could have won that race, but you didn't think it was polite to pass your boss.

Well, that's a good story. But what I would have liked to have done was get ahead of them and then stop, and wait, so they could win it! But I couldn't quite get there in time.

Talk about the year after that, when Bruce was killed and Denny got his hands burned and you stepped in for a few races. Tyler Alexander has said that you greatly helped to hold the McLaren team together.

It was really nice of Tyler to say that. Keeping the team going was the whole motive, really. Bruce was a larger-than-life guy. He had a great organization. He had such great plans for the future. He got snuffed out just when he was about to blossom even more. But I could feel that this great organization was on the brink of coming unglued. I felt, hey, you know, it's the sort of thing I would have expected him to do.

Bruce and I had struck up a pretty good relationship in terms of driver-to-driver, competitor-to-competitor. He drove our Eagle a couple of times, in Formula One.

I came in at Mosport, the first race that year. I always felt that Mosport was more European than any other track on this continent. It had more blind turns. It was more difficult to come to grips with. Therefore, I liked it a lot. It was like a small version of the Nurburgring.

I remember running a 465 engine in practice, but for the race there were no more 465s, so they put a 427 in my car. No big deal, but in the race, even though Denny had been burned pretty severely at Indy, he was still ahead of me. And he was being led by Jackie Oliver in the titanium Ti22 with a 495. Sort of an ill-handling car, but it really jumped. Denny could not accelerate with him, and Jackie was giving it a very, very good ride.

Finally Denny gave up, his hands were in such bad shape, and he waved me by. I thought, "What does he mean, me go get him? I'm already going as fast as I know how to go!" My tongue is hanging out like a necktie.

So I bore down some more. But though my car out-handled Jackie's, as soon as I got into his wake I'd lose the front end through the turns. Then on that uphill straight he could just open up five car-lengths.

At one point, he got a pretty bad start out of that Moss hairpin, and going up the straight I'm right behind him, in his draft big-time. I'm thinking, "I'm going to pop out about the time he's going to get to the top of the hill, and I'll just wheesh on by him on the inside." But something told me, "Uhhh, why don't you just not pop out, okay?" Some sixth sense. I didn't do it.

And Jackie went by a car that was parked on the racetrack, missed it by about three feet. If I had popped out . . . That was an interesting thing. Kind of chilling.

Finally, somebody put a little dirt on the road at the hairpin, and he made a big enough mistake that I got right up alongside of him, and I ended up on the cue ball position, inside going into the right-hander at the top, and got away from him.

But in the process, I set the new lap record that the F1 cars didn't beat the next year. That was fun.

If Big Dan had any preconception at Mosport 1970 that all he had to do was back up Hulme, Ollie in the No. 22 Ti22 soon straightened him out. Here the three blast out of Moss Corner—Gurney's the hot dog in the bun at the moment—and shape up to overwhelm Dick Durant's No. 81 Lola T163. *Pete Lyons*

Peter Bryant
on the Titanium Car

AS AN APPRENTICE RACING MECHANIC in England, Peter claims, he was a member of the Team Lotus Space Program. He goes on to tell of the day Colin Chapman's boys built a rocket and launched it from the shop floor through a skylight. It was not long afterward that young master Bryant left England. He came to America with John Surtees to race-prep a Ferrari sports car, and stayed. He had been working on Can-Am McLarens and Lolas for several years, self-teaching himself engineering all along, when he seized an opportunity to build a car of his own design.

The Titanium thing was a result of being Skip Scott's crew chief for the 1968 Can-Am with one of the Simoniz Lolas. Through him I met Ernest Kansler, who had a company called Autocoast. They were prototyping and building a new 30-foot offshore powerboat. He also was doing some car projects. Ernest Kansler was in effect Henry Ford's adopted great-grandson. He had a trust fund from his father, and I helped him spend it.

I said, 'Why don't we design and build a Can-Am car with the Autocoast name on it.' He was excited about that, and gave me the go-ahead.

That was the Ti22, which I designed, and we built it out of titanium—the chassis tub and the suspension. Bob Bondurant test-drove it for the first time at Orange County Raceway. Bob wanted to drive it, and we wanted Bob to drive it. But Ernie said that he wanted to see a European Grand Prix driver in it.

David York, the team manager for John Wyer, whom I knew very well, recommended Jackie Oliver. I contacted Oliver, and he didn't know who I was or anything, so I said, "Fly over. You can assess the car. If you don't like it, I've got another driver. If you like it, I'll pay you $1,000 a race against 40 percent of the prize money," which was a pretty good deal in those days, in 1969. So Jackie went over that car with a fine-tooth comb. He didn't know anything about titanium. When he picked up the pieces, he said, "Oh my God. This is really light." His eyes lit up. He knew we were on to something.

We tested the car at Willow Springs, then took it to Laguna Seca. We were late to the track. That was the worst moment of my entire life, driving across the bridge in the truck at Laguna. Chris Amon in the Ferrari and two McLarens went under the bridge, WANG-WANG-WANG. I thought, Oh my God. Look what you've done. You've designed a car, brought it to the track, and now you expect it's going to do that? I mean, I really felt bad. But a year or two later I spoke to Eric Broadley and he said, "Peter, every time I've designed a new car, I felt exactly the same thing." So that made me feel a little better.

Former Lotus mechanic Peter Bryant (left) came to America to work on Big Banger sports cars, and wound up creating his own. In the hands of F1 driver Jackie Oliver (right), Bryant's two Ti22 Titanium Cars of 1969-70 and his 1971-72 Mark 2/Mark 3 Shadows were among the strongest challenges McLaren ever faced. *Pete Lyons*

Race-ready only in time for Laguna Seca 1969, as shown here, the first Ti22 (a name derived from the chemical symbol and atomic weight for titanium) featured a wedge-shaped profile and full-length fences to create high downforce. By the next race the ambitious little team would add a finally popular strutted rear wing. *Pete Lyons*

We had lots of trouble with the throttle sticking and no trouble with anything else. We actually didn't qualify for the Laguna race. They put us on the back of the grid. Got up to 7th place from 31st. The titanium nut and bolt that holds the throttle cable to the pedal, apparently it wasn't a lock-nut and it came undone. The throttle cable come off. We had to put the nut and bolt back on. So we finished 13th.

Then came Riverside, where Oliver qualified fourth on the grid, and was battling for third in the race. The differential broke?

The bulkhead on the back of the car that held the top of the shock absorber had a titanium boss welded to the titanium bulkhead, and the weld broke. It sheered off. We couldn't announce to the press that the titanium broke, of course, because the Titanium Corporation of America was trying to get into sponsoring the car. Nobody could really see what it was under the body. We told them it was the differential.

That's what you told me. Thanks a lot.
You're welcome.

At the start of the 1970 season the car was fast again at Mosport, then it flipped at St. Jovite. You didn't get a replacement together until late that year.

The car was gronked after St. Jovite. I was designing the Mark II version. I already had developed the process to hydroform the bulkheads and the tooling for the second car. Now I had to make a decision—do I stop what I'm doing with the second car, or build another tub for the first car? There's 3,000 rivets in the tub. It took the Titanium Corporation two months to make all the panels.

So rather than try to put the first car back together, we actually turned the tub upside down and used it as a table for a barbecue at one of our mechanics' house. After that, we took it back to the workshop. It got in the way, so we stuck it outside. The trash truck picked it up and put it in the Newport dump. We were upset about it, and we went after it, but we couldn't find it. To this day it's probably still there, because titanium doesn't go rusty. It's probably got a fleet of houses built over it by now. Years from now when someone digs around, they'll find a titanium Ti22 chassis laying in the Newport dump.

Now we really had to crush on the second car, but I was running out of money. Ernie Kansler had told me that he wasn't going to sponsor a car anymore. I was approached by a syndicate of a lawyer, a doctor, and a guy that owned a machine shop. They said that they would like to run the Ti22. I had no choice. So I said okay. They started to fund the project, and we carried on and finished the car in time for the last two races, Laguna and Riverside.

Norris Industries sponsored the car. They gave us 10 grand a race. Ken Norris was a real nice guy. He told me, "Peter, I can't put my finger on it, but be very careful. Something weird is happening." After the Riverside race, the lawyer calls me up while I was in the workshop. He says, "Come

Bryant constructed his chassis tubs as well as suspension links and other parts out of light, strong, but hard-to-work Ti. After the original car was destroyed in a backflip early in 1970, Bryant hastened to complete a second-generation chassis in time for Laguna Seca that year (shown here). *Pete Lyons*

over to my office." So I went over to his office and went upstairs, and there they all were. He says, "Peter. We voted you out. You're no longer managing, running the team. We're taking over." He had this legal document that said that now he was running the team. I went into shock. I hyperventilated right in the office. He was sitting with his back to a big window. I contemplated pushing him and the desk through the window. I was so angry and upset; I think I could have done it. Then I thought, "No. No. No. You've got to do this with a lawyer." The last thing I said to him was, "You will never race this car." He said, "Oh yes, we will." I said, "No you won't. Because there's one small detail you forgot. I have a personal contract with Goodyear and the rest of these sponsors. They all belong to me. I'm going to take them to someone else. Or I'm going to get this car back. But you'll never race this car."

After Bryant lost control of his Ti22 project, the remaining Titanium Car was campaigned privately. David Hobbs gave it some strong runs, as here at Riverside 1971, but in the hands of a later driver it crashed and burned to the ground. *Bob Tronolone*

I actually had a paper that said I was the owner of the car, from when we took it to Canada. We started proceedings, but the lawyer I got wasn't as ruthless as she needed to be. But they couldn't get any sponsorship. They couldn't even get tires. They started to argue amongst themselves. One of them stole one of the engines from the workshop, took it to his house. They all fell out.

About a month into the design of the Shadow, I got a phone call from this guy who ran the machine shop. He said "Peter. We realize now that we made a terrible, terrible mistake. We would like you to come back. We'll give you 50 percent of the team and we'll run the car in the Can-Am." I said, "We'll talk about it." I got in my car. It was nine o'clock at night and I was driving up the freeway to Santa Fe Springs, and I said to myself, What are you doing? Screw me once, shame on you. Screw me twice, shame on me. I turned around and drove home again.

So I never helped. They went bankrupt. The car was auctioned off. Dean Moon bought the transporter, and Nick Dioguardi bought the car. Dioguardi didn't know anything about titanium cars. I guess he thought the car would last forever. He called me up, and I said, "I don't know what you're going to do with the car, but be careful. Because if you don't understand titanium and its foibles, you could have a real dangerous situation."

By the end of the Can-Am season, I had the Shadow racing against the Ti22. That was tough. David Hobbs was driving the Ti22. He did very well. He out-qualified us at Laguna Seca. But Oliver was much better in the race than during practice and got ahead in the race.

So after that, Dioguardi decided to drive it himself. He was in a club race at Riverside, something broke, and it crashed and it burnt to the ground. I mean it melted. It went right to the ground.

1971: Stewart and Lola Challenge McLaren

McLaren's Peter Revson Takes the Crown

When Can-Am series organizers partially limited the cars in 1970 (no "moving aerodynamic devices"), they hoped a more technologically level race track would attract a greater number of competitors.

In 1971, the two McLaren team drivers had just one significant competitor—Jackie Stewart. He won the F1 world championship in 1969, and would do so again this year plus a third time in 1973. His sheer speed was in not in doubt. Mounted in a McLaren, or an equivalent, he'd have been a solid Can-Am contender. As it turned out, the new factory Lola T260 he drove was not a McLaren equivalent, but "the Mod Scot" (so dubbed by the American press for his long hair) did win 2 races of the season's 10 and made most of the others interesting.

Stewart started out by taking pole position for round one at Mosport and led several laps of the race until his transmission failed. In St. Jovite's round two, he qualified second to Denny Hulme and eventually passed the defending champion to score a Lola's first win since 1967.

The racing looked better from behind the fences than it really was. Stewart was struggling with a narrow, blunt car that was a bullet on the straightaways, but lacked aerodynamic downforce for good cornering. Suspension development also seemed lacking. The white T260 handled, said Stewart famously, "like a pregnant elephant."

At the same time, the two Orange Elephant drivers—Hulme and his new partner, Peter Revson—were struggling too. It wasn't like McLaren, but the new M8Fs weren't quite up to speed when they arrived. New-boy Revson wasn't up to speed

American champion: Peter Revson became Hulme's teammate for 1971, and won 5 of the season's 10 races, to put the series trophy in U.S. hands for the first time. *Rich Mitter*

either; he was distracted at the time with McLaren's Indianapolis car program. At St. Jovite, Hulme faded midrace with a stomach bug.

Both Lola and McLaren worked hard on their cars during the season, but McLaren had more to work with. Based on the successful M8A design of 1968, the wedge-shaped M8F was following proven evolutionary lines. Lola's round-nosed T260 was an experiment in trading high downforce for low drag. As other teams had found over the years, it wasn't the way to fast Can-Am lap times. During the year more and more downforce was added, finally with a grotesque "cowcatcher" wing cantilevered out ahead. Lola kept making suspension revisions in the field, too.

None of it kept the car competitive. Stewart's second victory, at Mid-Ohio, came to him only because he drove very slowly on the bumpy track, avoiding the breakages that knocked out the two McLarens. That, too, was unlike McLaren, and remained so. Not that the McLaren team didn't have problems, some of them pretty dramatic, but only one other time did an M8F break down before the finish (Hulme's at Elkhart Lake). That totaled just three retirements in 20 starts. Stewart's lone Lola racked up 5 out of 10.

In the end, "Champagne Peter" Revson took five wins to Hulme's three, and became the first American Can-Am champion in the series' six seasons. Other teams did bring other new cars that year. A new Shadow was produced by former rivals

Winning smiles: Between them, Revson (left, 1971 champion), Stewart, and Hulme won every round of the series. The Can-Am was a driver's championship, and it did attract the best. Denny, two-time series winner, was also a former F1 World Champion. Jackie had already won that crown in 1969, would clinch it again this year, and again two years later. Revvie . . . who knows what he could have achieved? He had all it took but died young. *Pete Biro*

Don Nichols and "Titanium Car" designer Peter Bryant, using tires a step larger than the tiny ones of the first Shadow. Despite Jackie Oliver's hang-it-out driving, it wasn't competitive. Jo Siffert in a new version of his 1969 Porsche wasn't competitive either, although the underpowered car was again very reliable and again he finished fourth on points—sadly a posthumous distinction, because of an accident in F1. Ferrari made a single appearance, Mario Andretti driving a new 7.0-liter car. BRM came back for only two races. March never did return. As in all Can-Am seasons, privateer teams with obsolete machinery bulked out the fields. They often put on a good show. But winning meant beating McLaren. For five years, nobody had tried hard enough.

World champion challenger: Ever since Team McLaren began its Can-Am domination in 1967, it seldom lost a race, and never to a faster competitor. In 1971 Jackie Stewart and the all-new Lola T260 changed the equation. Stewart qualified on pole for the opening round at Mosport and won the second race at St. Jovite. Midseason he scored another pole and another victory, plus a fastest race lap. But the car broke as often as it finished, and it was always hard work to drive. The driver kept asking for more downforce, and by the end of the season Lola gave him an ungainly airfoil cantilevered out front (as shown at Riverside's Turn 7, with Oliver's Shadow Mark 2). Dubbed the "cow catcher," it wasn't the answer. *Pete Lyons*

Ready for anything: McLaren manager Teddy Mayer (left), mechanic/fabricator Alec Greaves, and crew chief Tyler Alexander direct the Riverside race—by eye, in the days before radios. These two ugly Americans (as Tyler referred to himself and Teddy) plus one of several handsome Englishmen were vital parts of this team, widely described as "Kiwis from New Zealand." *Pete Biro*

Flat out: The old Can-Am deserves to be remembered for the races that were hard-fought, like this one at scenic St. Jovite. Hulme (No. 5 McLaren M8F) started from pole, but Stewart (No. 1 Lola T260) relentlessly pushed and pushed until the normally indestructible Bear sagged with a tummy ache. *Pete Lyons*

Champ's ride: McLaren's M8F was yet another evolution of the 1968 model, though longer, wider, and with even more power. Inside the all-aluminum (no iron cylinder sleeves) Reynolds-block Chevy were 495 ci and something like 735 horsepower. Note the staggered-length intakes, which smoothed lumps in the power curve, and the full-length body fences, which added downforce. These were two of the reasons Can-Am cars were faster than F1s of the day. *Pete Lyons*

Maximum effort: "Ye must never let y'self fall into the habit o' drivin' at anythin' less than yer maximum!" Stewart once said. Lola head Eric Broadley (right) hired the Mod Scot for his ability to get the most out of a machine, and Jackie did put the difficult T260 into victory lane twice. But it was an effort the F1 champion chose not to repeat the following year. *Pete Lyons*

Fabulous 5-liters: The Can-Am was known for its big block Detroit "iron," but exotic, multicamshaft engines from Europe were welcome too. Here at Laguna Seca, Jim Adams in the ex-Amon Ferrari (now with a 5.0-liter V-12) cuts the hairpin ahead of Jo Siffert in the second-generation Porsche 917 flat-12 of the same displacement (still nonturbocharged). *Pete Lyons*

Second Shadow: Former Ti22 builder Peter Bryant (far right) joined forces with Don Nichols (holding clipboard) for a new Shadow with tires larger than before, though still not up to conventional sizes. The front wheels were 12 inches in diameter when the new team stopped off for a test session at Chaparral Cars' Rattlesnake Raceway in Texas en route to its first Can-Am—they were using Chaparral-built engines. Later the front wheels grew to 13 inches, still smaller than the 15s commonly used by other Can-Am cars. As with the original Shadow, the idea was a lower body profile for better top speed. *Michael Recca collection*

Dices within dices: Racing each other into the Laguna hairpin, Jackie Oliver (No. 101 Shadow), David Hobbs (No. 49 Ti22), and Brian Redman (No. 38 BRM P167, visible between them) also have to deal with the brake-locking Jerry Hodges (No. 25 Hodges/McKee) plus Roger McCaig (No. 55 McLaren M8C) and Gary Wilson (No. 18 McLaren M12). Whew! *Pete Lyons*

Mr. Oversteer: Jackie Oliver drove the Shadow Mark II with tremendous verve, as seen here at Riverside's Turn 6, and typically qualified fourth or fifth fastest. Once he qualified second overall. Unfortunately, the team only entered 8 of the season's 10 races, and the car lasted to the finish in just 2. At least Shadow was making progress compared to the year before. *Pete Lyons*

Magic bus: Denny and Revvie's prerace parade precisely forecast the Riverside result. After their "pace lap" in Gulf's vintage omnibus, the pair got into their modern Gulf McLarens and drove to a one-two victory. *Pete Lyons*

Pete at his peak: After five seasons, Peter Revson put a halt to the overseas flow of Can-Am gold. *Joanne Dearcopp*

Hodges LSR. The McKee "Wedgie," which introduced turbocharging in 1969, was back in 1971 with a supercharger. This time the blower was on a Chevy, rather than an Olds, and new owner-driver Jerry Hodges called his zoomie-looking hot rod the Hodges LSR. He only raced one Can-Am, Laguna Seca, where he qualified 27th and completed only 14 laps, due to ring-and-pinion failure. *Bob Tronolone*

Along with Jackie Oliver, Peter Bryant joined Don Nichols for 1971 and created an all-new Shadow. Make that almost all-new—apart from the rear wing of the original *Tiny Tire* car, Peter says he retained halves of two wheels. The Mark 2 Shadow started out black, but turned white in stages during the season. This was the color scheme at Elkhart Lake, where Ollie started on the front row. *Pete Lyons*

Peter Bryant on Shadow

AT THE END OF 1970, Bryant's Ti22 Titanium Car was snatched away by business partners. He fought back but, as he says, "You can't let grass grow under your feet," so he phoned across Los Angeles to fellow American Can-Am car builder Don Nichols.

Somehow, Don Nichols and I had been kind of converging. When we were building the Titanium Car, he heard about it. He had a van, and he used to pull up at my house in Costa Mesa, as we were building the tub in the driveway, and shoot pictures out the window. He was spying on us. But [original Shadow designer] Trevor Harris was a real close friend of mine, so I didn't have to spy on him. Trevor told me everything. "We're building this real radical small, low car."

So I said fine, I'm not going to go that route. It's too unconventional. I had seen on paper the footprints of the tires he was using. They were

When the Mark 2 Shadow first appeared at St. Jovite, proud papa Peter found himself giving an always-curious Hulme an insider's look at the 12-inch, low-profile front tires, and inboard brakes. *Pete Lyons*

wide and thin [thin in front to rear dimension] and I thought, well, it could work. But you couldn't put a 12-inch brake disc inside a 10-inch wheel. So he had to cut the brake disc down, and it didn't have any brakes. The driver had to sit with his feet like this [splayed out]. The coolers [engine radiator] were in the wing. With the small wheels, the wheel rpm was totally out of sync with anybody's gearbox. Everything had to be special on that car. It was way too trick. The thing went like a raped ape down the straightaway. But when it got to the corners...it was an interesting exercise as a concept car.

Don had asked me a couple of times, if ever you get free and you want to do something together, let me know. So I approached him and said, "Look. I've got this sponsorship with Goodyear, so why don't we do a newer version of the Shadow."

We went to Ohio and brought his old car back in secret, because everything with Don was done

To take further advantage of its low body line and to improve airflow to the rear wing, the Shadow used Chaparral-tuned engines complete with the old 2H/2J low-profile induction system. The body cross section also incorporated vestiges of the full-length fences Bryant had used on his Titanium Car. Monocoque panels were made of aluminum on this car, not Ti, but were black-anodized for hardness as well as the Shadow image (picture taken at Laguna Seca). *Bob Tronolone*

During 1971, Shadow went up a size to 13-inch front Goodyears, which required a slight readjustment of the front fender line. But adhesion was still a problem, even with fences added for more downforce, as here at Riverside. *Bob Tronolone*

in secret. In fact, when I was drawing the new car, we didn't want anybody to know who the pieces were being made for. So in the title block on the drawings we wrote Blivity Car Company.

We wanted a secret place to do this, so we rented a back office from an insurance agent on Atlantic Avenue in Long Beach. It was just one room. It was 10 by 8 feet. I had a drawing board that was 8 by 5 feet. There wasn't a lot of room left in the room. I had no telephone. After much struggle, Don agreed I could have a chair. I'd start work at 7 in the morning and I'd work until 7 or 8 at night. I started in, I think it was February, and the Can-Am was in June. So we had to hurry.

I was collecting unemployment, $100 a week. I couldn't quite live on that, so Don gave me another $100 with the understanding that if we got any sponsorship, I would be brought up to speed salary-wise. I can't remember if he finally paid it all or not. Don was good at getting people to give him credit.

Don said, "You must use as much of the old car as you can." I used one-half of the rear wheel. It was a 12-inch spun aluminum bolt-to-gether wheel, which had a big deep offset. I used it as the inside half of the front wheel. Because of the gearbox problem, we had 15-inch wheels on the back.

The only thing I brought from the Ti22 to the Shadow was titanium. The front suspension was all titanium. The rear suspension wasn't because most of that's machined, and titanium is really rough to machine. You need some strength in there too. The modulus of the titanium isn't as good as steel in certain applications. Also, titanium was too difficult to fabricate. Welding was a hit and miss thing. Sometimes, you'd just throw pieces away. You'd make a control arm, adjust it, and the end would break off. We didn't have the time.

Somehow we got tied in with UOP [Universal Oil Products], and they said they needed references. I spoke to Larry Truesdale at Goodyear, and he called Ben Williams at UOP and told him I had never been associated with an unsuccessful vehicle. On that say-so, UOP agreed to sponsor us.

Goodyear promised to do the tire development. They were worried about the 12-inch front tires being so small and the rpm being so high that they'd overheat, so they made the compounds too hard. We were wearing out the track. When we took temperatures, they weren't

Giving up on the idea of low frontal area in 1972, Shadow went to conventional tires on 15-inch-diameter wheels. Despite all the consequent changes, Bryant managed to construct this Mark 3 on the old Mark 2 chassis. *Bob Tronolone*

Shadow also spent 1972 trying to develop a turbocharged Chevrolet and made a second Mark 3 chassis with extra fuel capacity for it. Oliver finally tested this engine in public during the last Can-Am weekend at Riverside, but it wasn't ready to race. Crewmen are Barry Crowe (signaling driver), Graham Everett (at wing), and Lee Muir (touching door). Among the curious onlookers is Mark Donohue (folded arms at rear). *Michael Recca collection*

any hotter. We finally convinced them to start softening up on the compounds.

Midway we switched to 13-inch fronts. On the back they were 15-inch, but we had the first low-profile tires that Goodyear ever made. Those were 26-inch outside diameter, and the sidewalls were 3 inches high from the rim to the tread. Goodyear took the technology they got from the small tires for this car to Formula One. They really learned a lot from that Shadow.

We had real trouble with the wheels. At the end of the straightaway at Riverside, at about 220 miles per hour the centrifugal force pulled the tire away from the rim. Oliver was testing, and it did it twice. We had to bolt the tires to the rim, but the aluminum was too soft, we couldn't seal the things. Now they had more places to leak. Most of the tire trouble we had with that first Shadow was tires going down because the air leaked out. We never solved the problem.

What I should have done was cast some new wheels, but there wasn't time. You can barely get a drawing done in the racing season. You're doing everything with tape and putty.

For 1972, we used the same chassis, but went up to 15-inch wheels front and back and changed everything else. It was practically a new car [the 1972 Mark III]. We changed the bodywork three and a half or four times in the one season. You would find out more at each track. Whether it was a slow track or a fast track, it would require a different body configuration. If you couldn't get to the terminal velocity of the car, you'd use the horsepower to make downforce.

I used to carry sanding discs, and I'd stick them on the front spoiler. They were rough, so they would slow the air down going into the radiators. You would pick up 20 pounds of downforce. We used to play tricks like that and find out whether it worked. In the Can-Am days the name of the game was whatever works, do it.

Sometimes you'd do stuff just to screw the others. Didn't work, but you knew what it did because you'd tested it. So you put it on, do a hot lap. They'd all rush off and make one of those, you know?

One of the funniest ones was, we were at Mosport with this Shadow. We were going to try to turn a couple of real hot laps early in the qualifying to make people think, "Boy, these guys have really got it." So we took some pink paint and just put a little pink dot on all four tires.

The spies from McLaren and Penske, immediately you do a hot lap, they come look at your car. Penske's guys spotted this pink paint. Went to Goodyear and demanded they get a set of that qualifying rubber like Bryant.

Of course, nobody will back this up and say we did it. But we drove the Wiener [McLaren's Teddy Mayer] crazy.

In 1972, private Porsche driver Milt Minter scored equal points with championship runner-up Denny Hulme. Seen here at Edmonton, the turbocharged 917 was owned by import dealer and lifelong racer Vasek Polak (in jacket), and prepared by Alwin Springer (white shirt). Springer later operated his own racing enterprise, Andial, before Porsche appointed him U.S. motorsports manager. *Ozzie Lyons*

Alwin Springer

NOW DIRECTOR of Porsche's North American motorsports operation, Springer was crew chief on Vasek Polak's Can-Am team for driver Milt Minter, among others. He thus became intimately familiar with the mighty 917s.

I think for the time when that car was around, it was state of the art. The car by itself, the engine, the transmission; everything was good. If you didn't overrev the engine, we would get some good hours out of it, and even when you took it apart it wasn't like you had to replace so many parts. It was a very reliable engine.

The major downfall on the turbocars was when you would warm up the engine in the morning before the race. I was always crossing my fingers not to foul up the spark plugs. That's because the injection pump was a purely mechanical system. In today's world you have electronics, it's so nice now. But at that time it was a very, very tricky business. If you were not completely careful with it, it could be too rich and you could never get the misfire out. You would have to change the plugs, and that was one thing you did not want to do.

Is it true you had to take the engine out to change all 24 spark plugs?

No, no. But we had to do it from underneath the car. See, some of them you can't reach from above, and even from underneath the space is very, very small. So it was a major undertaking. In an emergency, you could change the plugs in two hours. Normal circumstances, five. You ask me what I remember most? Exactly that point!

How long to change the whole engine?

Normally, six hours. Under racing conditions, maybe three and a half. Because we had to lift the engine out of the car. You couldn't move it backwards, as with the McLarens, and you didn't have a lot of room to move around.

That's due to the aluminum-tube space frame. Was that a high-maintenance item?

No. I don't remember a cracked frame for anything besides an accident. Suspension; also aluminum, but they weren't as fragile as they are today.

The whole car, really, was low-maintenance. You have to remember, I did the whole season [1971 and 1972] with Milt and a helper and myself.

McLaren Specials

Mighty M8Bs—the McLaren lineup that won all 11 races of the 1969 series. *Pete Lyons*

BECAUSE MCLAREN REFUSED to sell its latest models to potential competitors, some customers tried on their own to come up with something better. The M6Bs modified in 1968 by Donohue/Penske and Gurney/Eagle (shown elsewhere), were two of the best known. Here are some other McLaren-based specials.

Goth McLaren. Starting with one of the first production McLarens, the pre-Can-Am M1A, Mike Goth (with help from Cobraman John Morton) fabricated this M1B-like body and drove it in several 1966 races. *Bob Tronolone*

Chaparral McLaren. While trying to get its radical model 2H race-ready in 1969, Chaparral Cars provided this modified M12 to John Surtees for several races, including this round at Bridgehampton. In addition to the strut-mounted, fixed-angle rear wing, which McLaren did not supply to customers, the car's aerodynamics benefited from a low-lying "crossover" engine induction system borrowed from the 2H. *Pete Lyons*

Leslie McLaren. Local man Ed Leslie competed in the 1970 Laguna Seca Can-Am with this M6-bodied, 6.0 Chevy-powered homebuilt. He qualified a very decent 17th in a field of 32 and lasted to finish 14th. *Bob Tronolone*

Spirit of Edmonton McLaren. This 1969 production model M12 enjoyed quite a long and varied life. In 1970, driven here at Mid-Ohio and elsewhere by Graeme Lawrence, it had "Batmobile" wing mounts and publicized the Can-Am in Canada. *Pete Lyons*

Dutton McLaren. A squared-off chassis, instead of the M6B's originally rounded lower sides, is just one of the aero tweaks that distinguished former Chaparral engineer Tom Dutton's modified McLaren in 1971. *Bob Tronolone*

Specials

Bruce McLaren (1968 McLaren M8A) founded the team that won more Can-Am races than any other. *Pete Lyons*

McLaren "M8R." That's in quotes because it's not a McLaren factory designation. Originally a wingless 1970 M8C production model, the car was updated to this high downforce configuration when Dick Durant drove it in 1974. *Dale von Trebra*

1972: Big Blown Banger

The Dawn of the Porsche Era

Beware of what you ask for. Can-Am fans had been wanting McLaren to have some serious opposition. But they didn't want the Orange Elephants to get blown out of the circus. That's exactly what the blowers on Porsche's 12-cylinder 917 engine did that year.

Porsche had been feeling out the Can-Am since 1969, when Jo Siffert first tried a roadster version of the mighty 917 Le Mans coupe. It was impressively reliable then and during a second season in 1971, enough so that Siffert twice took fourth place in the championship. But the 5.0-liter European racing thoroughbred simply couldn't match the brute power of "Detroit Iron" (actually aluminum by then) with half again as much displacement.

Bolting on a pair of turbochargers changed the equation. Whistling out nearly 1,000 horsepower and now driven by Mark Donohue and George Follmer for Roger Penske Racing, the 1972 Porsche 917/10K crushed the 750-horsepower McLaren-Chevies. Awestruck bystanders immediately dubbed it the Panzer. The complex car had many teething troubles, and it didn't win its first race. But it did win the next, plus five more of the season's nine. The McLaren factory team only won two. The Kiwis never came back.

Color shift: After five solid years of nearly solid orange McLaren front rows, the 1972 Can-Am had a new complexion. Porsche teamed with Penske to produce the "Panzers," turbocharged supercars that whistled out nearly 1,000 horsepower. Poor old Chevy-powered Team McLaren was overwhelmed not only in that respect, but also financially. The Kiwis battled bravely—and Denny Hulme did win two more Can-Ams, bringing his career total to 22. When two gleaming white 917/10Ks appeared here at Donnybrooke midseason, the old guard's place was no longer at the top of the pecking order. *Pete Lyons*

Of course, racing is never as simple as the bare results appear to indicate, and Bruce's boys did wage a stout battle. For the first time since 1968, they designed an all-new car, the McLaren M20. They pushed their naturally aspirated Chevrolet engines beyond previous limits—once to 9.26 liters, nearly a liter larger than normal, a then-incredible 565 ci. They also worked behind the scenes on a turbocharger program of their own. Denny Hulme won two races and two pole positions, defending champion Peter Revson took another pole, and between them they notched fastest lap in four races. Denny-the-Bear earned second place in the championship.

It was all to no avail against the relatively huge Porsche engineering department, which was estimated to have four times the funding. After five years of showing everyone how to go Can-Am racing, McLaren finally faced someone who had taken the lessons to heart.

Not that victory came easily to the Penske Porsche. Getting the world's first successful turbocharged road racing engine race-ready was an extreme challenge, one that nearly wasn't accomplished by the first race. In that race, once again held at Mosport, the car did start from pole and did go into an early lead, but it dropped back with turbo system trouble. The same problem recurred two races later, at Watkins Glen, in front of European journalists flown in by Porsche. That was where Hulme in his McLaren won for the second time.

The Porsche also occasionally broke suspension, transmission, or other parts, and on one infamous occasion, at Donnybrooke, a race was lost because the supercar sucked up all its fuel. Most crippling was the Road Atlanta testing accident that robbed Mark Donohue of his chance to win that year's Can-Am series. The renowned driver/engineer had played a giant role in the Panzer project and had put the car on pole for its

Porsche puzzle: Twelve horizontally opposed, fan-cooled cylinders, quadruple camshafts, dual ignition, and twin KKK turbos; the complex Panzer was powerful, but far from trouble-free. After the car's first victory, in the second race of the season, Porsche invited friends from Europe to Round 3, here at Watkins Glen. Not even the touch of Roger Penske himself (leaning over the right side of George Follmer's cockpit) could ward off global embarrassment—a fifth-place finish, two laps down. *Pete Lyons*

Fighting to the front: It's facile to say Porsche and Penske muscled their way to Can-Am dominance with power and money. The international team's personnel also devoted enormous ability, hard-won experience, and relentless determination. Mark Donohue spent most of a lonely year helping to develop the world's first successful road racing turbocharger system, then spent months struggling back from a nasty testing accident while watching his stand-in, George Follmer, drive to the championship. Donohue even had to give Follmer the title-clinching race victory here at Laguna Seca, where Mark is seen pitting his No. 6 917/10K during practice. The original Can-Am 917PA ("Porsche + Audi") of 1969 passes by with Sam Posey driving. *Pete Lyons*

Last attempt: For the season finale at Riverside, McLaren's engine shop hogged out one Chevy to a then-incredible 565 inches—9.26 liters. The "Big Bertha" engine lasted three hot laps in qualifying, lifting Hulme ahead of one Porsche and alongside the other onto the front row of the grid. With a normal 509-ci engine in the race, Denny immediately lost ground at the start—his McLaren M20 is completely hidden behind Follmer's leading Porsche in this picture—and eventually that engine broke down, too. Revson, behind Donohue here, did come home second, but then McLaren went home for good. *Pete Lyons*

Tweaking technology: Even privateers tried to meet the Turbo Porsche threat. Monte Shelton's aging Lola T162 (No. 57, on the outside line through Riverside's Turn 1) got a scoop-nose facelift and long tail fins just like the Panzer. Meanwhile, Denny Hulme (No. 5) got McLaren's first all-new Can-Am car since 1968. Actually designed for a turbocharged Chevrolet engine, though it didn't race with one that year, the M20 was longer, lighter, and sleeker. The driver also enjoyed stronger brakes and, thanks to side-mounted radiators, a cooler cockpit. The combination was almost enough. *Pete Lyons*

Powerful partnership: Roger Penske (left, on the Mosport pit counter) was a top-rank sports car driver himself, a member of the early Chaparral team as well as builder of his own "Zerex Special," an ex-F1 Cooper that figured in setting Can-Am rules, and in setting up Bruce McLaren as a constructor. But Roger's talents were even sharper in the business management role. Working together, he and driver-engineer Mark Donohue (right) built one of the most effective racing organizations of all time. *Lionel Birnbom*

first race. Just days before its second race, the rear body came loose at high speed and sent the magnesium tube-framed car tumbling to destruction. Mark was lucky to suffer injury only to a knee.

It hurt more to turn over "his" car to a stand-in. George Follmer, who had driven for Penske in the past, did a remarkable job of learning a difficult machine at very short notice. He qualified second fastest to Hulme at Atlanta, snatched the lead at the first corner, and after both McLarens went out (Hulme's in another Can-Am "blowover," a backflip cresting a rise), Follmer drove on to score the 917's first victory. After four more, George Follmer became the second American Can-Am Champ. Poor Mark Donohue came back to drive a second car in the last four rounds, but could only win one of them.

Two other constructors tried to make winning cars that year. Shadow returned with its 1971 model converted to full-size tires, and once again Jackie Oliver was stirring to watch. He qualified on the second row three times—once beating Hulme—and once finished second to

Through the esses: Riverside's signature was this sequence of high speed swerves, Turns 2 through 5. The rolley, slidey Can-Ams took them with a real flourish. Sam Posey leans on the No. 20 Porsche in the foreground, just behind Jackie Oliver (No. 102 Shadow Mk III), David Hobbs (No. 1 Lola T310), and Mike Parks (No. 13 Ferrari 512M coupe). *Pete Lyons*

Shadow take III: The third-generation car was actually the 1971 chassis, albeit with many changes, including high-downforce front body profiling, rear-mounted radiators, and, at last, full-size wheels. Front brakes were still inboard—note the inlet and outlet ducting. Otherwise, things were going about the same. Oliver qualified as high as fourth three times and finished a spirited second to Follmer's turbocar in the Mid-Ohio rain. He came third here at Donnybrooke. But out of nine green flags, the car was running at the checkered flag only twice. *Pete Lyons*

Follmer. Shadow was another Chevy-powered team trying to tame turbos and got as far as bringing the project out in public, though without result.

Lola had an all-new car, and the T310 really was new, a wide-track, high-downforce reversal of philosophy from the previous year. Also new was the driver, David Hobbs. He showed the car's potential several times, but once again Lola was doing its preseason development during the races. A lone fourth place was the best finish.

Though new cars fielded by their factories generally dominated Can-Am racing, privateers greatly contributed to the show and occasionally lucked into victory. French F1 star François Cevert drove a year-old McLaren M8F (Revson's former car) during 1972 and drove it hard and well. Twice he qualified fourth-fastest, and at Donnybrooke was there at the end when the factory McLarens and Porsches failed to finish.

It wasn't enough to keep McLaren in the series. At the end of the team's seventh Can-Am season, after 39 victories by factory drivers and five consecutive championships, manager Teddy Mayer made the financial decision not to compete with Porsche.

Alfa Romeo T33/4. A real crowd pleaser, this was another of the small enduro cars to take on the big sprint iron, although in this case Alfa's fine little four-cam, V-8 engine was bumped from three to four liters. California driver Scooter Patrick ran three Can-Ams in 1972. He qualified midpack, which meant ahead of many much bigger cars, and finished ninth, seventh, and ninth respectively, despite having to make midrace fuel stops. Later Milt Minter drove this car, while Patrick moved into McLarens. (He would win the very last Can-Am before the big-bore series died in 1974.) *Bob Tronolone*

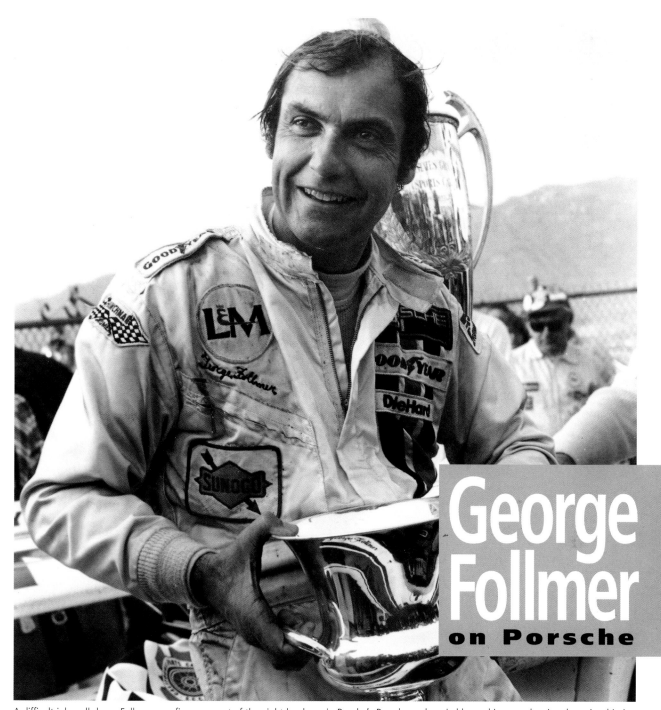

A difficult job well done: Follmer won five races out of the eight he drove in Penske's Porsche and carried home his second series championship in one year. *Bob Tronolone*

George Follmer
on Porsche

AFTER SPENDING several Can-Am seasons struggling with uncompetitive cars, in 1972 George Follmer was pursuing other opportunities. As a matter of fact, he'd just clinched the SCCA's Trans-Am championship when the phone rang. It was Roger Penske—for whom he'd driven as teammate to Mark Donohue in 1967—offering the greatest of Can-Am rides: the turbocharged, 900-horsepower Porsche Panzer 917/10K. Follmer drove it to that championship too. A reunion with the same car at Willow Springs in 1998 brought memories flowing.

Mark had his accident in testing at Road Atlanta, and Roger ran me down, and at 5:30 in the morning he had me in a rental car driving the track, because I had never seen Road Atlanta before. So I didn't know the track, and I didn't know the car, and I got thrown in with Denny Hulme and Peter Revson. You know, a couple of wolves that were very hungry in McLaren M20s. They were tough. That was kind of a real scary weekend.

So I had a lot to learn. I didn't know squat, I mean I was lucky to find the key to turn it on. Mark had already been testing the car almost a year, so he knew it real well, and he had it set up his way.

How hard was it to handle?

It was somewhat of a difficult car to drive. It did have some unusual characteristics. It was very short-coupled, a real short wheelbase. That was the biggest detriment to the car's handling. With the suddenness of the power you had to have it going the right direction. You had to be ready to go and you had to be ready to correct it, because it would come out on you. It did everything quick. It would accelerate quick, and it would twitch quick.

I would say it was at its best on the tighter tracks. High speed-wise, it was not fun. Places like Turn Nine at Riverside, you'd probably make three corners out of that. You'd have to walk it through—work the steering wheel all the way. It was real hard to get it just right.

Because of the turbo lag, you had to do everything before you wanted to. That was probably the biggest learning curve, having enough confidence in what the chassis was going to do, so you could tell yourself to put the throttle down. Anticipation is the best word for it. Everything you did in this car, you had to be already down the road with it. But the car had a lot of power, and it would go down the straightaway. If you drove it properly and got the boost up coming off the corners, it would light the tires real easy. You didn't lift off when that happened, because you didn't want to lose the boost, so you just kept your foot down, just left two big black marks.

One time at Riverside, I had the front end come up on me, maybe about 18 inches, out of Turn Six. I did let off then, and it came back down. It was just one of those cars you had to be on top of all the time.

But Mark was a lot of help, and the more I drove the car, the more I got confidence in myself, and confidence in understanding the car, and knowing what I could do, and what I couldn't do with it. I got very quick with it. At the end I would say, realistically, I was probably quicker than Mark was. Just, you know, being used to it.

That was the first successful turbocharged engine in road racing. How did you have to drive it?

One thing you had to remember, you didn't want to foul a plug. Because they were impossible to get at, and there were 24 of them. That's why on the pace laps we were going up and down, up and down, to keep the plugs blown out. If you just motored

The Panzer used its enormous power not so much for straight line speed, though it showed a lot of that, but to overcome the drag of a huge rear wing and high-downforce bodywork. That helped a lot in fast corners, but despite that advantage Follmer found the short-wheelbase 917/10K had skittery handling—yet turbo lag meant that he had to keep his throttle foot down no matter what. *Pete Lyons*

around there, by the time you did two laps you'd be dead. Once the motor was hot and if you kept the boost up, they were fine.

About 8,200 [rpm] was our redline, and we'd shift them right in there. You wanted to make your shifts good enough, so you didn't lose boost. You liked to keep it above 7,000 all the time, but sometimes you couldn't because it was only a four-speed. When you lost the boost it was a normally aspirated 5.4, and to me that's just a starter motor!

Ideally, in most circumstances, you'd be through braking and have already put your foot back on the throttle at the beginning of the corner, because it took some distance before you got full power back.

You couldn't left-foot brake to keep your right foot on the gas?

No, the steering wheel was in the way, and anyway it had synchros in the gearbox, so when you shifted you had to use the clutch. Your right foot was your throttle and your brake.

The shifting was hard. The gears were big and heavy. I always used to develop a big callous on my palm. The steering was kind of stiff, too, especially at high speed, because of the downforce.

But the cockpit didn't get as hot as a monocoque Can-Am car. And it was a real quiet engine, not as noisy as a big block Chevy. Brakes were good. It was reliable. It really was a pretty nice race car —made me a lot of money!

Yes, you won Atlanta, your first time out.

Danny out-qualified me by a couple of hundredths—it was real close. So he was on pole, I was second, and Peter was third. But they dropped the flag, I was in the corner first. Then Denny flipped and Peter broke, and I could spend the rest of the day learning how to drive this race car. That was easier on me.

Then came Watkins Glen.

That was positively our worst weekend. I didn't know the car well enough, and Watkins Glen's fast, so the wing factors came in. We got too much rear wing in it and it made the front push, and that tore up the front tires, so I had to keep waitin' for it to turn. Going up the Esses there, I'd just turn the son-of-a-bitch and nothing would

A case of opposites forced together, rather than attracted, Follmer (right) and Donohue were true rivals who had to work as a team to the end of the season. *Pete Lyons*

happen, because the faster the car went the more downpressure it had on the rear, and the lighter the nose got.

I just didn't know. I hadn't had enough time in the car; I had never tested. So I just looked bad. Denny and Peter both kicked my butt. I was third on the grid.

In the race, we had that relief spring that allowed it to, I guess, to idle. I'm not sure what it did, but Mark had the same trouble in Mosport, remember, the first race? We thought they had it handled, and then I had it at Watkins Glen and had to stop to fix it.

And of course that was the race the factory had brought all the European press. Well, that was a bad day at Black Rock as far as Penske's efforts were concerned. He looked bad, I looked bad, they were gonna fire my ass. You know, if the car doesn't win it's the driver.

They changed the car around a lot for Mid-Ohio, and it went better.

Oh, we tried different things all the time. Mid-Ohio, we had a bigger Goodyear tire for the back. They were trying to make the car go faster, and it did, though you could still light the tires up.

And that's where we changed the pickup points on the rear shocks, because where you come over those humps at Mid-Ohio the car would bottom out. Fortunately it was an aluminum-tube frame, so they could cut the pickup points off and weld 'em back on overnight. That was a benefit of the space frame, and it was a

Thrown to the wolves, George Follmer agreed to stand in for the injured Mark Donohue at Road Atlanta (where he's leading Denny Hulme's McLaren M20). That simply meant learning the world's most powerful and complex race car while driving against the reigning Can-Am champions on a high-speed track that he'd never seen. *Bill Warner*

benefit of having a Penske-backed operation. If the car needed something, it got it.

Then in the race it rained.

And Penske wouldn't let me come in.

He wouldn't let you?

You know the Captain, and his penchant for doing the right thing at the right time. That is up 'til 1998! But seriously, it started to rain and this car was a handful in the dry, but you put it on slicks on a greasy track and you've *really* got yourself a thrill. But I'd come by the pits and I'd look over at Penske, and he's just giving me a little wave, "Keep goin', keep goin'."

No radios in those days.

I was ready to give him the finger! Denny came in and got rain tires, and Peter and, I think, François Cevert did too. Pretty soon they came back out and just stomped my ass. I mean, they'd go by me like I'm tied to a fencepost. I couldn't do anything about it.

Jackie Oliver in the Shadow stayed on slicks, but he was catching you in the rain as well.

Jackie was pretty brave in rain, hell of a lot faster than I was. Shit, I was motoring around in fourth gear trying to keep the wheels from spinning. I did loop it. Didn't tear anything up, which was fortunate. Came by the pits again, and the Captain's standing out there, "Keep goin' . . ." I kept looking at him, "You've *got to be kidding*. Good God, man, do you want to go for a ride? I'll stop and you can drive it!" It was diabolical.

And goddamn if it didn't start drying out. Mid-Ohio, those showers come and they dump, and they're gone. I guess Penske, having been raised in Cleveland, maybe he had a feeling for it. So everybody else had to stop again for slicks, and we just went on and kicked ass.

But jeez, it was a handful in the rain.

When Donohue recovered enough to drive later that season, were you then the second driver?

Well, I had so many points in the series that I had to go on and win it, because there was no way Mark could make up enough points for the races he'd lost against Denny and Peter. If it hadn't been that situation, I'm sure that Mark would have jumped in the car and I would have been standing there watching.

So that worked out real well, and having two of us out there was a lot of fun, because I could race Mark one-on-one. I had to have a good car, because I had to win races too. And actually I did. I drove a lot for Roger off and on, and I have to say, he always gave you a good car. It may have been the second car, but it was still a good car. His second car is probably better than a lot of first cars.

In his book, The Unfair Advantage, Mark described a feeling of loss when his accident forced him to give another driver this supercar that he had spent so much time developing. You said he did help you, but do you think he withheld anything?

Well, he probably didn't withhold anything 'til he got back in. [Laughs] Then it might have changed. I know for a fact a couple of times he had a new engine, and I had his engine from the race before in my car. I was running the second engines at Laguna Seca and Riverside. Riverside, I was faster. I mean I out-qualified him and I out-ran him. Laguna, he had power all over me. That was like the third-generation engine for the season. It was a 5.4 and it was real strong.

I didn't realize Porsche ran the 5.4-liter in 1972.

We got the 5.4s about halfway through the season, I think. I might have had a five-liter at

Laguna, but I know the 5.4 was there then and he had the 5.4 in his car.

How was the 5.4 different to drive from the 5.0?

Just more torque and more power. I think the horsepower jumped two, three hundred from the beginning of the season. Because we were running them about one and a half bars on the boost, and we could go more. You sometimes did.

How much more?

[Whispering] We never told anybody.

It's 25 years, George!

Well, somebody might be listening!

Oh, I've had it up there to 1.6, 1.7. Just for a short time. Sometimes you'd get some backmarker that's got a good engine down the straightaway, but he holds you up in the corners. Well, when you hold me up in the corners with this car, and I come off at a lower boost, then I don't have that luxury to go blasting by like you do with a big block. So sometimes to compensate and get by somebody, we'd give it a little twist. We probably had 1,200 horsepower at times, if we wanted it.

You drove the 917/10K again in 1973, and you won a race, but you had to watch Donohue win six in the 917/30.

The 917/30 had a longer wheelbase, so it would get through high-speed corners. Mark had me there, but I could keep up on tighter stuff. The 10, get it on a tight track, I could be pretty competitive with a 30, or even the McLarens.

The McLaren M20 was a long-wheelbase car, and it handled very well. In 1972, had McLaren not had to press the engines so far to keep up with us on horsepower, they probably would have won some more races than they did, because some places they were quicker chassis.

Was the 917/30's main advantage its longer wheelbase, or were there other things?

Oh, it was aerodynamically cleaner, the weight distribution was better, the suspension was different. Everything that they learned in 1972, they adopted on the 1973 car. It may have been the "same motor," quote, but it certainly was a hell of a lot better car.

Was it still as good on tighter corners?

Yeah, it didn't give up anything. It was just easier to drive all the way around. It was more predictable and more stable. With the 10, like I say, in fast corners you might have to correct a couple times, and while you're doing that, you obviously don't have your foot buried in it. If you feel stable and you know the car's going to stick, like Mark did with the 30, you hit the throttle sooner and *PSCHTT*, it's gone.

People at the time were saying Mark and the 30 were, quote, "The most perfect combination of man and machine ever seen."

Oh, I think anybody could have driven it. It was a good car. I mean Brian Redman drove it well against us in the Shadows at Mid-Ohio in 1974. Mark certainly complemented it, and it was designed with an awful lot of his feedback. One of Mark's big advantages was that he was able to interpret what the car was doing, and make it do what he wanted. A lot of drivers can't. So when he prepared his cars, they'd be for him, and he didn't have to drive ten-tenths all the time to accomplish something. Some of the rest of us had to make up in driving what we didn't have in the car.

That's what made Mark, Mark, really.

Driving a leftover 1972 car, now privately owned and updated as much as possible, Follmer pedaled as hard as he knew how during 1973. At Mid-Ohio he forced his way in front and held off Donohue for many laps. But the Super Panzer finally prevailed. *Daniel Lipetz*

1973: Porsche Perfect

Penske's Panzer Thoroughly Dominates

In its eighth year, the Can-Am was a story of one man, and one car. Mark Donohue, the American engineer who drove Germany's turbocharged Porsche to competitiveness the year before, finally got to drive it to the championship.

Coincidentally, this eighth season included only eight races. It was enough. Donohue did have trouble with the new, blue Porsche 917/30 in the first two events, but the supercar was fully sorted by round three, and from that point on, Mark was totally dominant. He drove alone for the Penske team, and no effective rivals emerged from other teams.

In short, the Can-Am was as dull this season as its outside critics had long claimed—except for the deep pleasure racing enthusiasts take in watching perfection in action. The car Mark called "a monument to my career" was a thoroughly revamped version of the previous year's 917/10K. The 30 had a longer wheelbase, revised suspension geometry, a stiffer chassis frame, and more efficient bodywork. More power, too. Its 5.4-liter, twin-turbo 12 normally raced with as much as 1,200 horsepower, and in excess of 1,500 horsepower was available if necessary.

It wasn't. McLaren had quit the series, as had Lola, and the only remaining factory, Shadow, wasn't competitive. The new Penske car's only opposition came from

Trying again: Despite three seasons of struggle, Shadowman Don Nichols refused to give up his Can-Am dream. Now also tackling F1, he opened a factory in England and had designer Tony Southgate create an all-new Shadow sports racer. The massive DN2 was intended to house a turbocharged Chevy, but one of the few times that monster motor ran was here at Laguna Seca in Vic Elford's hands. Leaping through the Corkscrew just behind is privateer Bob Nagle (No. 17, 1971-model Lola T260). *Pete Biro*

Pummeled Panzer: Just to remind us that, no matter how the results lists look, racing is never easy. Mark Donohue's 1,200-horsepower Porsche 917/30 may have been the one great car of the year, but he still had to find the finish line. At Mosport, here, somebody got in his way. Next time out, the problem was fuel spraying into his lap. "Captain Nice" worked hard for his Can-Am championship. Joe Rusz/Road & Track

River of power: Big-Banger sports car racing was born and bred here at Riverside, and reached glorious maturity in the Can-Am. But now critics were saying the all-conquering Turbo Porsche was too much of a good thing. Was interest in the series dying? Count the crowd. Pete Lyons

year-old or older cars. Best among them were a handful of privately owned 917/10Ks, some of which had the 5.4 engine but none of which had the 917/30's handling.

Two of them did have more luck, at least in the first two races. Though Donohue started Mosport from pole, he went off-course while lapping a backmarker and body damage dropped the SuperPanzer to seventh. Early challenger Jody Scheckter and third-fastest qualifier George Follmer dropped out, so Follmer teammate Charlie Kemp scored a Can-Am win. All were in Porsches.

The picture looked much the same at Road Atlanta, except that Donohue's problem this time was a fuel leak, and the first man past the checker was defending race winner and series champion Follmer.

Then came Watkins Glen, and Mid-Ohio, and . . . and all the rest of Mark Donohue's (and Porsche's) winning season, all practically picture-perfect.

Class of one: With the Porsche's problems finally ironed out, Donohue finished the season with six straight victories, a unique achievement appreciated by everyone. Those greeting him in the Riverside winner's circle included mechanics (from left, riding) Heinz Hofer, Greg Seifert, and Woody Woodard, plus Penske PR manager Dan Luginbuhl (in necktie), series official Berdie Martin, and second-place driver Hurley Haywood. *Bob Tronolone*

Face of a champion: Victories do not come without sacrifice. Mark Donohue had suffered much, including the dissolution of his family life. As he donned his laurels at Riverside, he was preparing to announce his retirement. *Bob Tronolone*

Porsche SP20. While all eyes were on the mighty 12-cylinder turbo Panzers, at the other end of the scale was Hanns Muller-Perschl's little special powered by a six-cylinder Porsche. He only appeared at Riverside, where he qualified at the back of the pack. That's where he finished, too, but at least his was one of eight cars still running. *Pete Lyons*

Mario Andretti

THE EXTRAORDINARY MARIO ANDRETTI raced nearly everything and won just about everywhere. But he never got a fair chance in the Can-Am. He appeared in only 20 of the series' 71 events, and due to mechanical troubles actually started only 14 races, finishing just 6. However, those finishes included a third place, two fourths, and a fifth. Once, in 1969 at Texas World Speedway, he qualified second fastest—splitting the factory McLarens—and led the first few laps until the car quit. Had Mario ever driven decent equipment, he certainly would have been a major contender. But failure is especially instructive in motorsports, and his unsatisfactory experiences cast a lot of light on the old Can-Am.

If there's anything I feel I missed in my career, it was a good Can-Am ride. That was fierce racing. But doing Indy car full time, there was never really room for a proper Can-Am effort. I always wound up with a half-assed situation that was more of a frustration than anything else. Some

Mario was hard pressed to show his best in *Honker II*, an ill-handling Ford project of 1967 which he began racing here at Bridgehampton. The car was made in England, but campaigned by Ford's Holman Moody stock car team. *Honker* was the nickname of John Holman, who loved to drive big-rig trucks. *Pete Lyons*

Mario Andretti didn't get many Can-Am rides, and few of them were good, but he always got the most out of them. At Watkins Glen 1971 he put the monstrous 7.0-liter Ferrari 712M fifth on the grid and fourth under the flag. *Pete Lyons*

The first time Andretti ever saw *Honker II* was in practice for Elkhart Lake, where he was nonplused to find the gear shift lever on his left. Worse, it didn't shift the gears properly. He didn't race the car that weekend. *Pete Lyons*

kind of weird phenomenon coming out of Ford, or some other kind of a concoction to try. They were all crazy cars that didn't amount to anything, because there was no real good engineering involved.

Your first Can-Am race was Riverside 1966, driving a Lola T70 with a big Ford 427 and an automatic transmission.

Yeah, that's the point. I wanted to have something normal, just a straightforward Hewland four-speed, which they were in those days, and go racing. But Ford, they're trying to emulate the Chaparral.

Quite honestly, I was not ready anyway. I didn't have the experience for proper road racing, not to that level. If I ever felt out of my element, it was that. I remember every time I came in I had a chunk of tire hanging on my fender. The course markers in those days were half-tires, and I always used to slice my apexes really tight, BANG! I'd come in and Eric Broadley would say, "Mario, tsk-tsk, you need more experience." In those days I didn't accept that, but he was so right.

The following year Ford built a car of its own in England, the Honker II. It did have a manual gearbox, but it was never one of your favorites.

Ha-ha. The Honker was just a total, total disaster. I'll tell you, to bring the Honker to Elkhart Lake for me to drive on a race weekend without testing . . .

Unbeknownst to me it had a shifter on the left-hand side, which didn't really even work. The linkage, from the middle console, had to go through some 90 degree angles to clear the engine, and the joints were going over-center and giving me wrong gears. One of the British guys said, "Well, you must get used to it." "Get used to it!" I said, "I'm in the right slot, it's not giving me the gear!"

They redid the shifter, but the car still was a disaster. We never had enough development to feel comfortable with it. There was always something. As soon as we got it going fast, the thing wouldn't stop. And look at all the aerodynamics on the other cars. I was losing out in the high-speed turns, big time.

You had some real horsepower in 1969 with the "429er," the year-old McLaren M6B with a 494 Ford engine.

It was incredible. The thing was so powerful. But just brute power, almost uncontrollable power. It was not nice to drive, not driver-friendly by any means. It came on so hard, and you had no real throttle feel, it was almost like a toggle switch. And narrow power-band; coming off the corner you'd hit it, BWAAAAHH, the thing [the massive power rush] would happen, but then there was nothing left. The explosion was gone.

Andretti

They didn't need to have that, but in those days that's what they all wanted, big muscle. But it was a learning curve for everybody. Uncharted waters. And, ah, Ford felt very free to experiment with me.

You did lead the last race of the season, in Texas.

I led until I blistered the right-side tires. You had to do part of the speedway banking, and the thing had so damn much power I was building up a lot of speed, and those road racing tires just started blistering and chunking. Probably we should have had a little more negative [camber] on the right side, but it was lack of testing and everything else.

It was an older chassis, but it was capable of winning there. You could really stretch your legs at that place. That was probably the only good moment I had in the Can-Am.

These later Ford-engined cars had manual gearboxes, but behind the scenes they kept working on an automatic. Did that have some good points?

No. Zero. I mean, the thing was scary. If you stuck a throttle you couldn't even get it into neutral, because it didn't have a neutral.

I forget which one it was, but at Stardust in Las Vegas we were testing this crazy gearbox, and they had this huge engine, like a 500-incher. It probably had 700 pounds-feet of torque. The ports were so big, at a quarter-throttle it was like having full throttle. What we were trying to work out was a compound throttle, where it wouldn't open up the butterflies so quickly [to wide open throttle], so it had all kinds of linkages in it and was sticking all the time.

One day I'm going down the straightway and I back off, and the thing sticks. I'm so busy I don't get my hand on the ignition until I'm maybe three, four hundred feet out into the desert. I hit some boulders. No big deal, cosmetic damage only, but I figure enough of this shit, and I walk back to the pits. One of the mechanics says, "I'll go get the car."

Well, I forgot to tell him that as soon as he turns the ignition on, the engine will fire, the throttle is down, and the thing is in gear! You know, because there's no neutral. I'm running after him, waving my arms, but meanwhile he hits the switch. It's like a big explosion. All the dust, the wheels are spinning, he hits some more boulders—oh, it was so funny! I mean, he could have killed himself, but it turned out okay.

How was that seven-liter Ferrari 712M you raced at Watkins Glen in 1971?

It didn't drive like a Ferrari. The car was never tested, it was just kind of an impromptu,

On the good side, *Honker II* launched Andretti's long friendship with movie star and race driver Paul Newman (in striped shirts), whose name appeared on the car. "Why don't we put my name on and let him drive?" Mario suggested plaintively here at Bridgehampton. *Pete Biro*

169

Mario's expression indicates that whatever he was hearing from Ludovico Scarfiotti (left) at Bridgehampton 1967 wasn't helping, but at least they were speaking the same language. *Pete Lyons*

Andretti

One of Ford's more promising projects was a modified McLaren M6B built in 1969 by Holman Moody. Though the engine was an all-aluminum, hemi-head giant of 494 ci (8.1 liters), the biggest in the Can-Am at that time, the car was known as the "429er" to publicize Ford's latest production powertrain. Andretti was reasonably competitive with this McLaren special and actually led the season finale in Texas. It is shown on its debut in the pit lane at Elkhart Lake and in winged form atop Laguna Seca's Corkscrew. *Pete Lyons*

throw-it-together, "Yeah, that's what we need." But it wasn't.

Ferrari didn't have a good feel for seven-liter engines, they really didn't. You could tell it was brand new, and that there was a lot of stuff missing. It probably didn't really have the power that it could have had, the thing was not smooth, it had some holes in the power curve, hesitations in the throttle; things like that. It was okay, but it needed to be developed.

But it was not going to be a winner, because the chassis flexed so much. In those days Can-Am cars were already monocoque chassis, but this was still tubular, and very thin tubing. A flexi-flier isn't necessarily something that's bad, but there's a point that, whenever a car doesn't repeat from corner to corner, then you know it's deflecting too much. This huge chassis with the huge package of the engine, I don't think the rear end knew what the hell the front end was doing. That car was diabolical in that respect.

But you'd be surprised: just a few gussets in the frame, and it might really have come alive.

Your last Can-Am effort was a few races in 1973, when you had a year-old McLaren M20 with a turbocharged Chevy.

Oh, yeah, the turbocharged thing. I liked that car, actually, that was the best chassis that I had driven. It was just more up to date, more aerodynamically correct. That was fun to drive. But the engine had a huge, huge turbo lag.

One of Andretti's least favorite cars was 1971's Ferrari 712M, which arrived at Watkins Glen untested, and performed accordingly. Mario never asked to drive it again. *Pete Lyons*

Andretti

"A freakin' airplane engine" is how Mario remembers the musclebound turbocharged Chevy in the McLaren M20 he drove in 1973 (shown slicing through Riverside's Turn 7), but he liked the car's handling. With enough development—and enough time—who knows how strong he might have been against the Turbo Porsches? *Pete Lyons*

See, they were always going for peak, they were not thinking of the flexibility need of the engine. All they needed was to downsize the turbos like four times and lose about 200 horsepower, and we would have had probably two and a half seconds better lap times! I don't need this freakin' airplane engine back there. But they were always reaching for the stars.

We were testing that car at Riverside, and I asked one of the mechanics to go along. I couldn't get him to understand what I meant, and I thought maybe he could share with me the feel of this huge turbo lag. The poor guy! He was so petrified, he had no idea what was going on. I said, "You see that?" He was goin' "Huhhh...?" Just vacant. So that was not very constructive.

It should have been more flexible, but the thing had power. I tell ya what, on that straightway—oh, man!

Two times you started heat races in that M20, then gave it to John Cannon for the finals.

I was totally disgusted, yeah. I didn't have any affection for that car because, you know, I'm lookin' like an idiot, I have no chance. It was hard for me to give up at any time, but this was enough. And I think he was going to continue the development, so might as well give him an opening; have at it.

Unfortunately, I always seemed to be driving an older chassis like that year-old McLaren in 1969. You look at the new ones Hulme and McLaren were driving, how beautiful, how state-of-the-art, even in those days. *Today* that car looks right, you know? So here I was half psyched-out just by looking at what the hell I had to run up against.

So I missed out big as a driver when it comes to the Can-Am.

1974: Long Shadows

The Curtain Closes on the Can-Am

Mercifully, it was over quickly. The Can-Am was going for eight races again this year, but it died at five. Diagnosis: terminal ennui.

Of many great shames about the great old series, one is that Shadow didn't get it right until this season. It did get it right, the new Shadow DN4-Chevy being quick and well developed, and hard-charger Jackie Oliver finally winning not only races but the championship. If Don Nichols' team had been as well organized, prepared, and armed in any of the preceding years, its competitive flame might have kept the Can-Am alive.

Instead, by 1974 nobody cared. Crowds, sponsorship, and participation had all been trending down anyway, the economy was soft, and automakers previously known for performance were preoccupied with safety and environmental concerns. Then the world "energy crisis" led Can-Am officials to impose fuel consumption limits. Porsche understood this to be an attempt to curb the power of its Panzer and canceled its planned third season.

In fact, Penske brought out the 917/30 for one race, round four at Mid-Ohio, a tight track where the turbocar could get its best gas mileage. As Mark Donohue had temporarily retired, Brian Redman drove. He drove beautifully, beating Shadow

The last Can-Am: In fact, this "Shadow Showdown" at Watkins Glen came in October, six weeks after the old series died prematurely in August after only five rounds. Jackie Oliver had taken the championship with four first places in a row. New teammate George Follmer claimed that he wasn't permitted to win and vented his frustration in this 15-lap grudge race, held during the U.S. Grand Prix weekend, by blowing away both Oliver (No. 101, at left) and Shadow F1 driver Jean-Pierre Jarier (No. 102). *Michael Recca collection*

Always game for a new challenge, Follmer tackled a real one in the 1970 *Tiny Tire* AVS Shadow. Its ultralow body profile yielded high top speeds, as intended, but nothing else about the highly unconventional machine was competitive. The little wheels jumped off the road over bumps, the little brakes faded, and there were big engine radiator problems. After struggling at Mosport (here) and St. Jovite, George decided to look for another line of driving work. *Pete Lyons*

Panzer defeated: Porsche quit the Can-Am after two years of domination when SCCA imposed new fuel consumption rules designed in part to curb its power. However, because Mid-Ohio was the least fuelish track on the schedule, Penske brought the 917/30 out one more time with Brian Redman driving. He qualified fastest, but the raceday rain didn't mix well with the selected tires. *Jim Chambers*

drivers Oliver and George Follmer out of pole and racing with them in damp conditions until his specially grooved front tires faded.

Critics have dubbed the Porsche "the car that killed the Can-Am," but others might question whether the famous Panzer could have saved the series by contesting the next race. It didn't, and on Monday after Elkhart Lake, the remainder of the season was canceled. Ironically, Shadow had fallen on its face there, both cars breaking down and leaving what turned out to be a final Can-Am victory to—trumpets, please—a McLaren. However, Scooter Patrick's M20 was a two-year-old privateer entry. It was a well-prepared and well-driven two-year-old car, but leftovers weren't what Can-Am fans craved.

"The George and Ollie Show" was what remained etched into people's memory from the last season. There may only have been one front-rank team to watch, but it was worth watching. In adding Follmer to its strength, Shadow gave Oliver a partner more competitive than expected. Unlike the old Bruce and Denny days, these teammates were not the best of friends. In fact, physical confrontations occurred both on- and off-track.

But when they were simply driving hard against each other, hurling around the turns and blasting up the straightaways, shaking the very earth, their brawny Black Elephants with their bellowing Big Bangers left an indelible image of what Can-Am racing was all about.

Don Nichols' team finally came good in 1974, with a new Shadow DN4 that was light, well balanced, and reliable. Ironically, this was the year that Porsche and Penske abandoned the Can-Am, leaving Shadow as the only full-scale factory entrant against the remaining ranks of privateers with aging Lolas and McLarens. At least the Ollie and George Show was a genuine scrap, the teammates letting their real personal animosity show on the track. Here at another rainy Mid-Ohio, they literally beat on each other. *Jim Chambers*

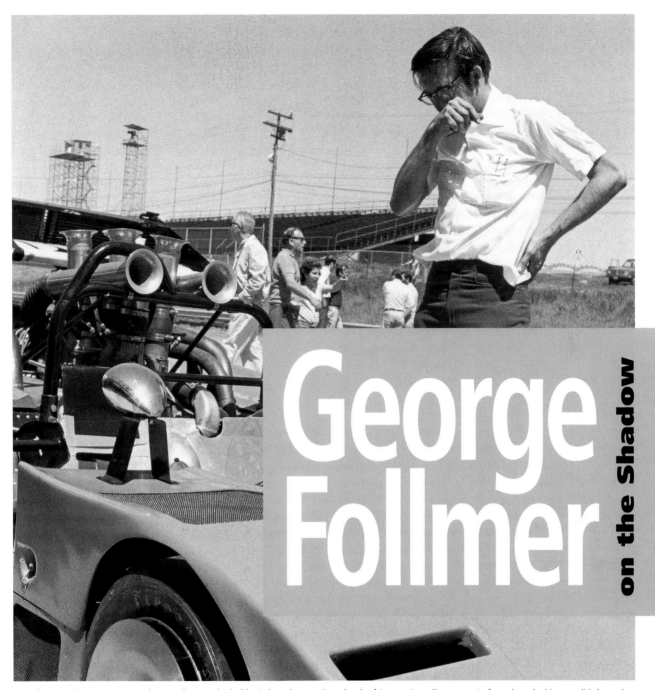

AVS designer Trevor Harris may be wondering why he'd tried to chew such a chunk of innovation all at once. In fact, though this one didn't work, such wild experiments are exactly why the old "unlimited" Can-Am remains such a legend. And don't worry about clever Trevor—he rose above this to build many winners. *Pete Lyons*

George Follmer on the Shadow

TWO YEARS AFTER EARNING the 1972 Can-Am title in Penske's Porsche Panzer, Follmer joined Shadow alongside eventual 1974 champion Jackie Oliver. That was Follmer's second time with Don Nichols' organization. Beginning in 1969, he extensively tested the original "Tiny Tire" AVS Shadow designed by Trevor Harris, and then was first to race the radical low-profile vehicle at Mosport and St. Jovite in 1970.

There was something that'd get your attention! Total panic city. Oh, it was tough. But it'd go down the straightaway. The theory was there;

177

Four years after his first experience with Shadow, Follmer came back to a much better race car, but an unsatisfactory team setup. George maintains that he was the faster driver but had orders to let longtime Shadow leading man Jackie Oliver win the races. That's how it turned out in 1974 (as here at Watkins Glen, where Jackie's No. 101 DN4 leads), although Follmer (No. 1) did run into a number of problems—and, on one occasion, into Oliver. *Bill Oursler*

Trevor had a good theory as far as small frontal area. Don didn't have any money for engines, so we never had a big motor, but at Mosport it went down the straightaway as fast or faster than any of the big boys. But you got to the corner, and it was another story. It wouldn't stop. Maybe two laps and then the brakes were gone. And it didn't corner. You know we had no shocks. We had those friction shocks. They'd work if you cranked 'em down tight enough, but then it'd just hop across the road.

When you rejoined the team four years later, Shadow had changed to a completely conventional car, Tony Southgate's DN4.

That was an awful good car. Docile. Quick. It cornered well, and it was slippery, clean, fast. We had good power—we didn't have near what the Porsche had, but it was normally aspirated, so you could get it on real quick.

With a turbocar you've got to come off the corner good. If a guy blocks you, one of these moving chicanes that park in the corner and rocketship down the straightaway, it's hard to pass unless you anticipate—hang back going in, set him up and get a run at him. But with a normally aspirated car you could chase a guy through the corner and just muscle him.

At that point I think the Shadow was a better car than the Porsche. The car complemented me, or I complemented it, or whatever, but it felt good. I was comfortable in it, and I enjoyed running it. It was a fun car to drive. Still one of the best I ever sat in.

It wasn't a happy year for you, though. To begin with, just before the first race there was a crash that hurt your back.

I had broken ribs. Yeah, I used to go to the doctors and get Lidocain spinal blocks before I drove. Remember, we ran pretty short heat-races in 1974. If I timed it just right, and there weren't a lot of yellows, I'd be OK for the 45 minutes it usually took the race to go. When the spinal block would wear off, I'd finish the race, but I couldn't *race*.

So that was frustrating, and the politics was frustrating. Terribly frustrating. You know, everything was controlled. They were going to give Oliver that championship whether he earned it or not. They didn't care where I qualified, but I had to let Oliver win.

Did you know that going in?

No. Not originally. At Mosport, the first race of the year, I won the first heat, so I was up front for the second start. Oliver had something happen to his car and was at the back. So I'm sitting in the car on the grid, and Don came up and told me I had to let Oliver win.

I didn't like that.

Was there any connection to your altercation with Oliver in the garage between the heats?

No, not really. What happened there, I asked Oliver what happened to his car in the first heat, because I didn't know at the time. And he took offense to it. He says, "Mind your own damn business," or "Get out of my face," whatever. And I didn't appreciate being talked to like that.

Follmer

So you took a swing at him?

Ah, he ran, the little, little bastard. Because I probably woulda killed him if I'd caught him. [Chuckling] I'd still be beatin' on him.

Then at Mid-Ohio, where Brian Redman challenged you both in the Porsche, you and Oliver hit each other on the track.

Oh, I just got pissed off, because he kept blocking me, so I wound up sustaining damage. Well what did I have to lose? I was supposed to let him win anyhow, so what difference did it make? People thought I took myself out of that race. Well, yeah, I probably did, but I would just as soon have taken him off and let Brian win! [Bitter laugh]

It was a frustrating year, and the crew was frustrated too. The guys that worked on my car knew that they couldn't win. Well, hey, mechanics deserve to win too. They put in an awful lot of effort to their cars, and their efforts are primary to whether the car wins, or finishes, or doesn't finish.

Remember the Grudge Race?

Oh, among the three Shadows at Watkins Glen at the end of the year?

Was it three of us? Yeah, I guess it was. What was it, a 10-lapper or something like that, winner take all, $10,000, and it didn't count for points. So I could race. Well they dropped the flag and I was gone. By the end of the first lap I had four or five seconds on Oliver.

I remember how exhilarated you were at the end. You were saying, "Nobody can drive a Group Seven car like I can."

Oh, yeah, I could actually go and win a race! It was a new experience.

The greatest—or at least most action-packed—race of that short last season was Mid-Ohio, where Redman's Porsche (No. 66) held off the Shadows for a while, and then Oliver (No. 101) held off Follmer (No. 1). George finally retired his badly battered DN4 and stomped away in frustration. *Daniel Lipetz*

Jackie Oliver

Oliver made Can-Am history with the Bryant Ti22 at Mosport 1970 when he gave McLaren's Dan Gurney a real fight. *Pete Biro*

NOSTALGIA IS SOMETHING THAT doesn't interest him, Oliver says. Like many racers, he's focused on the present, and what he's going to do next. He doesn't much remember or care about what he's done in the past.

So it's left to us to remember "Ollie" as one of the most exciting drivers to watch in the old Can-Am. He burst onto the scene in 1969 with Peter Bryant's neat little Ti22 "Titanium Car," and soon put it right up with the mighty McLarens. Then at St. Jovite he put the car on its head, fortunately without personal injury. For 1971 he and Bryant moved to Don Nichols' Shadow team and began another long struggle toward the front.

Whether his car was competitive or not, Jackie always had his foot in it, and you always knew that one day, with just a skosh more power, or road holding, or luck, he was going to win. That day came in 1974, when Oliver won the first four of the season's five races to became the seventh and last driver to be champion of the old Big Banger series.

"I remember that!" he admits.

The Can-Am was a great series. I mean, it had a tremendous following. They were big-bruiser sports cars, and they were quick, spectacular, and sounded terrific. It was primarily an engine series, big horsepower. And there was the ability within the regulations to innovate—Jim Hall's Chaparral team, for example.

The cars were fun to drive because you could unstick the back end. They had a lot of brute force, a lot of torque. I love torque. But they were actually quite crude. They were enormous, heavy cars that would come unstuck quite easily. They were square, with a short wheelbase, and you couldn't get a nice smooth slide. Nervous cars, twitchy, edgy. Today, you could build a car that would beat them easily with half the power.

Peter Bryant's car was very light and stiff, because all the monocoque panels were made of titanium. Otherwise it was conventional, a strong, conventional car. I was able to give chase to the McLarens, but that's all, I was only able to hang onto the back of them. Our engine didn't have the same power, the traction wasn't as good, and McLaren and Hulme were two very good drivers. I certainly wasn't the best driver in the world . . .

My flip at St. Jovite in 1970 was at a hump that used to be there in the return straight. You follow someone over a hump-back hill, and you're in their turbulence so you have no downforce. As the road drops away, the car is still going up, and the air gets underneath and it takes off. The heaviest part of the car is in the back, 60 percent, so it drops down, and the front keeps going up, and there's nothing you can do about it. I remember thinking, What's happening? but it was all over very quickly—two seconds? It went all the way over backward. It did come down on its wheels in the end, but it destroyed the car and gave me a bit of a thud. I wasn't hurt at all, but I was bloody sore.

Later on, Peter and I joined together with Don Nichols on the Shadow project. Don was a very good salesman, and his business acumen was very good. He used to collate his ideas very well. He put the program together, and the concept was neat, wasn't it? The black cars with the cloaked figure going back to the old Shadow radio program of the 1940s. He created the team, the image, the name, and everything, and it was very good, no doubt about it.

I came in after the first small-wheeled Shadow car. I never drove that, I wouldn't get into it. That concept was, Let's make it all-American, let's use aerospace people from California who don't

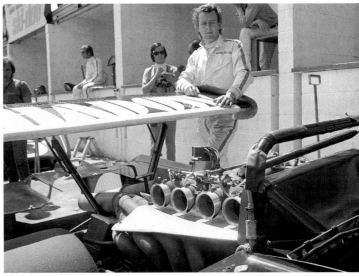

A Lotus F1 driver and winner of major endurance races with Ford and Porsche, Oliver expected better results from the Shadow in 1971. He'd have to wait for 1974. *Pete Lyons*

need to report to anyone or listen to anyone's advice. Let's come up with a completely novel approach, completely nonconventional. The result was, the small-wheeled Shadow was ill-fated. It didn't work.

Don spoke to me about it, and I said, "You ought to do it the right way, and that's not the right way." You want a conventional car. This trick stuff might be very appealing, and it may be exciting to pitch the sponsor with sketches of exotic cars, but in my experience in racing it never, ever worked.

Peter's approach was completely different. He was an opportunistic race mechanic, basically. He had some engineering qualifications in college,

Shadow founder Don Nichols (right), Peter Bryant, and Oliver refused to give up. *Michael Recca collection*

Ollie serves notice that if the new Shadow doesn't beat McLaren, he's got a backup weapon! *Pete Lyons*

and he read a lot, talked with people a lot, and he picked up the craft of designing and building a race car. He had a born gift for designing, and he'd follow a logical approach in hiring, and he'd talk and listen and look at other things to make sure he didn't make any mistakes.

The Shadow he built for 1971, and which was further developed for 1972, was a fundamentally good car.

That was when the decision was made to turbocharge the big Chev. That was awful. Very crudely done in an engine shop in Chicago. It had an *eeenoooormous* amount of power, but it was much slower than the normally aspirated one, because it had tremendous lag. It used to come in with an enormous wallop, *Bang!* and light the rear wheels up in almost any gear—very exciting.

But the torque curve was peaky, I mean it was shaped like a roof, and no sooner would it come on strong than it would expire at higher revs. It was just a lack of knowledge of what it takes. It was very poorly engineered. I was very nervous about driving it, actually, because it produced such violent horsepower so instantaneously. I wondered if it was going to just snap everything. It was an absolute beast.

After that we moved to England, because we were also going Formula One, and Tony Southgate was our designer, a good designer. Aerodynamically, he was superior to anyone else. A lot of people copied his ideas.

Tony did two Can-Am cars for us. There was the DN2 in 1973, and, uhm, I don't remember that car at all. Then we started over for 1974, and designed and built the DN4 from the ground up just for Can-Am, without any compromises, and that was a much better car. That was the one that won the championship, my only championship.

It was a tremendous competition between George Follmer and myself. Great rivalry, like always when you've got teammates with the same cars. I think probably George felt that he was an American driving for an American team, so he should be Number One. I know he used to try and persuade Don that he should get the best equipment, the best engine. But it was a British driver and a British car, in fact, that was winning.

George chased me around the garage once, at Mosport. I said some smart-ass remark, I suppose. You know, when you're in front you always come up with a quip to make someone look ridiculous. He was going to pop me one. My major defense was to run like hell!

I'd try to psyche him out in the races. At Mid-Ohio, tight circuit, that race was pretty closely fought. George, try as

As did others who tested early turbocharged engines, Oliver found Shadow's 1972 version had plenty of peak power, but poor raceability. *Bob Tronolone*

he will, couldn't get on top of me. He was completely frustrated by me. He just kept hitting me from behind, crashing into me. All he succeeded in doing was damaging his own car, actually destroyed all the radiator ducts and the thing overheated. He came into the pits halfway through the race, and he was blowing steam. He got out of the car and left without saying a word to anybody. Ha-ha!

That race was the only time we had any real competition, when Brian Redman came in with the Penske Porsche for that one race, and we beat it. That was pleasing, and it added a little bit more credibility to the championship.

There were very few paid professional drivers in the Can-Am. There was a large private entry. Some were good, some less so. I didn't have any particular problem with them, but their approach was amateurish. You could see that when you drove against them. They weren't prepared to risk either themselves or their car, because they'd have to pay for it. Or they might have had a lack of confidence, perhaps. Who knows. But they could be easily intimidated. Closely fought battles were easily conceded.

There was a certain aura of lack of sophistication at the races. The crowd used to go for the event. Pitch the tent, drink a beer, have a party was part of the culture of the Can-Am crowd. There weren't so many real enthusiasts there, they were more party-goers having a good time. Especially at Watkins Glen!

At the time I was doing the Can-Am, it was the time of people power, flower power, California, all that. Spectator participation, where audiences tend to participate in the sport, really started there. At the start of the race, there was always the flasher, some guy charging around naked. And there was always a parade, and people waving banners. We didn't have that in Europe.

The trouble with that series is that it wasn't very well contested. You had few teams that could actually get the job done. The reason was the need for money. There are very few professional teams in the world anyway; you can count them on your toes and fingers. There's lots of people who buy cars and enter races, but there are very few professional teams who make, design, and build race cars and also test them. The majority of them are in Formula One. The Can-Am was an appealing series, but probably it was a bit too adventurous for the North American racing market at that time.

Designed for a turbo engine that never worked, 1973's DN2 was bulky, heavy, and hard to steer. That's from contemporary accounts; Oliver said he doesn't even remember the car. *Pete Biro*

Famous from any angle, the Oliver vs. Follmer battle at Mid-Ohio resulted in the fourth win in a row for No. 101 and the seventh Can-Am champion in the series' nine-year history. *Daniel Lipetz*

Appendix
Can-Am Year-By-Year Results

1966
Round 1 Results
St. Jovite, September 11, 1966
1. John Surtees (Lola T70-Chevrolet), 75 laps of 2.65 miles = 198.75 miles in 2.06:51.0, 94.014 mph
2. Bruce McLaren (McLaren M1B-Chevrolet), 75 laps
3. Chris Amon (McLaren M1B-Chevrolet), 74
4. John Cannon (McLaren M1B-Chevrolet), 73
5. George Follmer (Lola T70-Ford), 73

Round 2 Results
Bridgehampton, September 18, 1966
1. Dan Gurney (Lola T70-Ford), 70 laps of 2.85 miles = 199.5 miles in 1.53:22.42, 105.58 mph (record)
2. Chris Amon (McLaren M1B-Chevrolet), 70 laps
3. Bruce McLaren (McLaren M1B-Chevrolet), 70
4. Phil Hill (Chaparral 2E-Chevrolet), 70
5. Mark Donohue (Lola T70-Chevrolet), 69

Round 3 Results
Mosport, September 25, 1966
1. Mark Donohue (Lola T70-Chevrolet), 85 laps of 2.459 miles = 209.15 miles in 1.54:51.89, 109.25 mph (record)
2. Phil Hill (Chaparral 2E-Chevrolet), 83 laps
3. Chuck Parsons (McLaren M1B-Chevrolet), 82
4. Earl Jones (McLaren M1B-Chevrolet), 80
5. Paul Hawkins (Lola T70-Chevrolet), 79

Round 4 Results
Laguna Seca, October 16, 1966
Heat One Results
1. Phil Hill (Chaparral 2E-Chevrolet), 53 laps of 1.9 miles = 98.3 miles in 1.01:29.9, 100.7 mph
2. Jim Hall (Chaparral 2E-Chevrolet), 53 laps
3. Bruce McLaren (McLaren M1B-Chevrolet), 53
4. John Surtees (Lola T70-Chevrolet), 53
5. Denny Hulme (Lola T70-Chevrolet), 53

Heat Two Results
1. Parnelli Jones (Lola T70-Chevrolet), 53 laps of 1.9 miles = 100.7 miles in 1.01:22.2, 98.9 mph
2. Phil Hill, 53
3. Jim Hall, 53
4. Mark Donohue, 53
5. Bruce McLaren, 53

Overall Positions
1. Phil Hill, 106 laps
2. Jim Hall, 106
3. Bruce McLaren, 106
4. Mark Donohue, 105
5. Masten Gregory, 103

Round 5 Results
Riverside, October 30, 1966
1. John Surtees (Lola T70-Chevrolet), 62 laps of 3.275 miles = 203.05 miles in 1.53:59.5, 106.864 mph
2. Jim Hall (Chaparral 2E-Chevrolet), 62 laps
3. Graham Hill (Lola-Chevrolet), 62
4. Mark Donohue (Lola T70-Chevrolet), 62
5. George Follmer (Lola Mk2-Chevrolet), 61

Round 6 Results
Las Vegas, November 11, 1966
1. John Surtees (Lola T70-Chevrolet), 70 laps of 3.0 miles = 210 miles in 1.55:27.5, 109.25 mph
2. Bruce McLaren (McLaren M1B-Chevrolet), 70 laps
3. Mark Donohue (Lola T70-Chevrolet), 69
4. Peter Revson (McLaren-Ford), 68
5. Lothar Motschenbacher (McLaren-Chevrolet), 68

Final Point Standings 1966
1.	John Surtees	27
2.	Mark Donohue	21
3.	Bruce McLaren	20
4.	Phil Hill	18
5.	Jim Hall	12
6.	Chris Amon	10
7.	Dan Gurney	9
8.	Chuck Parsons	6
9.	Graham Hill *	4
10.	John Cannon	4
	George Follmer	4
	Peter Revson	4
13.	Earl Jones	3
14.	Masten Gregory	2
	Paul Hawkins	2
	Lothar Motschenbacher	2
17.	Eppie Wietzes	1
	Jerry Titus	1

*Ties for position resolved by drivers' finishing records throughout the season.

1967
Round 1 Results
Elkhart Lake, September 3, 1967
1. Denny Hulme (McLaren M6A-Chevrolet) 50 laps of 4.0 miles = 200 miles in 1.54:53.0, 104.454 mph
2. Mark Donohue (Lola T70 Mk3B-Chevrolet), 50
3. John Surtees (Lola T70 Mk3B-Chevrolet), 50
4. Jim Hall (Chaparral 2G-Chevrolet), 49
5. Skip Scott (McLaren M1C-Chevrolet), 49

Round 2 Results
Bridgehampton, September 17, 1967
1. Denny Hulme (McLaren M6A-Chevrolet) 70 laps of 2.85 miles = 200 miles in 1.50:07.6, 109.73 mph
2. Bruce McLaren (McLaren M6A-Chevrolet), 70
3. George Follmer (Lola T70 Mk3-Chevrolet), 69
4. John Surtees (Lola T70 Mk3B-Chevrolet), 69
5. Lothar Motschenbacher (Lola T70-Chevrolet), 68

Round 3 Results
Mosport, September 23, 1967
1. Denny Hulme (McLaren M6A-Chevrolet) 80 laps of 2.46 miles = 196.720 miles in 1.51:25.7, 109.93 mph
2. Bruce McLaren (McLaren M6A-Chevrolet), 80

3. Mike Spence (McLaren M1B-Chevrolet), 79
4. Peter Revson (Lola T70 Mk3B-Chevrolet), 79
5. Roger McCluskey (Lola T70-Chevrolet), 79

Round 4 Results
Laguna Seca, October 15, 1967
1. Bruce McLaren (McLaren M6A-Chevrolet), 106 laps of 1.9 miles = 201.4 miles in 1.58:55.33, 101.613 mph
2. Jim Hall (Chaparral 2G-Chevrolet), 105 laps
3. George Follmer (Lola T70 Mk3-Chevrolet), 104
4. Bud Morley (Lola T70-Chevrolet), 103
5. Chris Amon (Ferrari P4), 102

Round 5 Results
Riverside, October 29, 1967
1. Bruce McLaren (McLaren M6A-Chevrolet), 62 laps of 3.275 miles = 201.4 miles in 1.46:28.7, 114.406 mph
2. Jim Hall (Chaparral 2G-Chevrolet), 62 laps
3. Mark Donohue (Lola T70 Mk3B-Chevrolet), 61
4. Parnelli Jones (Lola T70-Ford), 61
5. Mike Spence (McLaren M1B-Chevrolet), 61

Round 6 Results
Las Vegas, November 12, 1967
1. John Surtees (Lola T70 Mk3B-Chevrolet), 70 laps of 3.0 miles = 210 miles in 1.52:05.5, 112.41 mph
2. Mark Donohue (Lola T70 Mk3B-Chevrolet), 70
3. Mike Spence (McLaren M1B-Chevrolet), 70
4. Charlie Hayes (McKee-Olds), 69
5. Bud Morley (Lola T70-Chevrolet), 66
6. Rick Muther (Lola T70-Chevrolet),

Final Point Standings 1967
1. Bruce McLaren 30
2. Denny Hulme 27
3. John Surtees 16
4. Mark Donohue 16
5. Jim Hall 15
6. George Follmer 10
   Mike Spence 10
8. Bud Morley 5
9. Charlie Hayes 3
   Parnelli Jones 3
   Peter Revson 3
12. Skip Scott 2
    Lothar Motschenbacher 2
    Chris Amon 2
15. Bill Eve 1
    Chuck Parsons 1
    Jerry Hansen 1
    Rick Muther 1

1968
Round 1 Results
Elkhart Lake, September 1, 1968
1. Denny Hulme (McLaren M8A-Chevrolet), 50 laps of 4.0 miles = 200 miles in 2.06:55.8, 94.540 mph
2. Bruce McLaren (McLaren M8A-Chevrolet), 50
3. Mark Donohue (McLaren M6B-Chevrolet), 50
4. Peter Revson (McLaren M6B-Ford), 50
5. Jim Hall (Chaparral 2G-Chevrolet), 49

Round 2 Results
Bridgehampton, September 9, 1968
1. Mark Donohue (McLaren M6B-Chevrolet), 70 laps of 2.85 miles = 200 miles in 1.47:34.30, 111.32 mph
2. Jim Hall (Chaparral 2G-Chevrolet), 70 laps
3. Lothar Motschenbacher (McLaren M6B-Ford), 68
4. Swede Savage (Lola T160-Ford), 65
5. Richard Brown (McLaren M6B-Chevrolet), 63

Round 3 Results
Edmonton, September, 29, 1968
1. Denny Hulme (McLaren M8A-Chevrolet), 80 laps of 2.527 miles = 202.16 miles in 1.57:37.7, 103.15 mph
2. Bruce McLaren (McLaren M8A-Chevrolet), 80
3. Mark Donohue (McLaren M6B-Chevrolet), 80
4. Sam Posey (Lola T160-Chevrolet), 76
5. Chuck Parsons (Lola T160-Chevrolet), 74

Round 4 Results
Laguna Seca, October 13, 1968
1. John Cannon (McLaren M1B-Chevrolet), 80 laps of 1.9 miles = 152 miles in 1.46:24.6, 85.6 mph
2. Denny Hulme (McLaren M8A-Chevrolet), 79 laps
3. George Eaton (McLaren M1C-Ford), 79
4. Lothar Motschenbacher (McLaren M6B-Ford), 79
5. Bruce McLaren (McLaren M8A-Chevrolet), 79

Round 5 Results
Riverside, October 27, 1968
1. Bruce McLaren (McLaren M8A-Chevrolet), 62 laps of 3.275 miles = 203.05 miles in 1.46:32.3, 114.353 mph
2. Mark Donohue (McLaren M6B-Chevrolet), 62
3. Jim Hall (Chaparral 2G-Chevrolet), 61
4. Lothar Motschenbacher (McLaren M6B-Ford), 60
5. Denny Hulme (McLaren M8A-Chevrolet), 59

Round 6 Results
Las Vegas, November 11, 1968
1. Denny Hulme (McLaren M8A-Chevrolet), 70 laps of 3.0 miles = 210 miles in 1.52:15.38, 113.1 mph (record)
2. George Follmer (Lola T70-Ford), 70 laps
3. Jerry Titus (McLaren M6B-Chevrolet), 70
4. Chuck Parsons (Lola T160-Chevrolet), 69
5. Sam Posey (Lola T160-Chevrolet), 69

Final Point Standings 1968
1. Denny Hulme 35
2. Bruce McLaren 24
3. Mark Donohue 23
4. Jim Hall 12
5. Lothar Motschenbacher 11
6. John Cannon 10
7. George Follmer 6
. Jerry Titus+ 5
9. Sam Posey 5
   Chuck Parsons 5
11. George Eaton 4
12. Peter Revson 3
    Swede Savage 3
14. Dick Brown 2
15. Dan Gurney 1
    Charlie Hayes 1

+ Titus awarded eighth place because of his third-place finish at Las Vegas.

1969
Round 1 Results
Mosport, June 1, 1969
1. Bruce McLaren (McLaren M8B-Chevrolet), 80 laps of 2.46 miles = 197 miles in 1.51:27.3, 105.90 mph
2. Denny Hulme (McLaren M8B-Chevrolet), 80 laps
3. John Surtees (McLaren M12-Chevrolet), 80
4. John Cordts (McLaren M1C-Chevrolet), 76
5. Chuck Parsons (Lola-Chevrolet), 76

Round 2 Results
St. Jovite, June 15, 1969
1. Denny Hulme (McLaren M8B-Chevrolet), 60 laps of 2.65 miles = 159 miles in 1.37:52.0, 97.55 mph
2. Bruce McLaren (McLaren M8B-Chevrolet), 60 laps

3. Chuck Parsons (Lola T163-Chevrolet) 59
4. Lothar Motschenbacher (McLaren M12-Chevrolet), 58
5. John Cordts (McLaren M6B-Chevrolet), 58

Round 3 Results
Watkins Glen, July 13, 1969
1. Bruce McLaren (McLaren M8B-Chevrolet), 87 laps of 2.3 miles = 200.1 miles in 1.35:17.6, 125.99 mph
2. Denny Hulme (McLaren M8B-Chevrolet), 87 laps
3. Chris Amon (Ferrari 612P), 87 laps
4. George Eaton (McLaren M12-Chevrolet), 84
5. Chuck Parsons (Lola T163-Chevrolet) 83

Round 4 Results
Edmonton, July 27, 1969
1. Denny Hulme (McLaren-Chevrolet M8B), 80 laps of 2.527 miles = 202.16 miles in 1.56:34.8, 104.35 mph
2. Chris Amon (Ferrari 612P), 80 laps
3. George Eaton (McLaren M12-Chevrolet), 77
4. John Surtees (Chaparral 2H-Chevrolet), 76
5. Tom Dutton (Lola T70 Mk3B-Chevrolet), 73

Round 5 Results
Mid-Ohio, August 17, 1969
1. Denny Hulme (McLaren M8B-Chevrolet), 80 laps of 2.4 miles = 192 miles in 2.02:16.6, 94.212 mph
2. Bruce McLaren (McLaren M8B-Chevrolet), 80
3. Chris Amon (Ferrari 612P), 79
4. Jo Siffert (Porsche 917PA), 79
5. John Surtees (Chaparral 2H-Chevrolet), 78

Round 6 Results
Elkhart Lake, August 31, 1969
1. Bruce McLaren (McLaren M8B-Chevrolet), 50 laps of 4.0 miles = 200 miles in 1.51:39, 107.479 mph
2. Denny Hulme (McLaren M8B-Chevrolet), 50
3. Chuck Parsons (Lola T163-Chevrolet), 49
4. Peter Revson (Lola T163-Chevrolet), 49
5. Tony Dean (Porsche 908), 47

Round 7 Results
Bridgehampton, September 14, 1969
1. Denny Hulme (McLaren M8B-Chevrolet), 70 laps of 2.85 miles = 199.5 miles in 1.45:40.58, 118.949 mph (record)
2. Bruce McLaren (McLaren M8B-Chevrolet), 70
3. Jo Siffert (Porsche 917PA), 70
4. Lothar Motschenbacher (McLaren M12-Chevrolet), 67
5. Pedro Rodriguez (Ferrari 312P), 66

Round 8 Results
Michigan, September 28, 1969
1. Bruce McLaren (McLaren M8B-Chevrolet), 65 laps of 3.0 miles = 195 miles in 1.48:14.09, 109.098 mph
2. Denny Hulme (McLaren M8B-Chevrolet), 65 laps
3. Dan Gurney (McLaren M8B-Chevrolet), 65
4. Jo Siffert (Porsche 917PA), 64
5. Andrea de Adamich (McLaren M12-Chevrolet), 63

Round 9 Results
Laguna Seca, October 12, 1969
1. Bruce McLaren (McLaren M8B-Chevrolet), 80 laps of 1.9 miles = 152 miles in 1.27:29.77, 104.8 mph
2. Denny Hulme (McLaren M8B-Chevrolet), 80 laps
3. Chuck Parsons (Lola T163-Chevrolet), 80
4. Mario Andretti (McLaren M6B-Ford), 80
5. Jo Siffert (Porsche 917PA), 79

Round 10 Results
Riverside, October 26, 1969
1. Denny Hulme (McLaren M8B-Chevrolet), 61 laps of 3.3 miles = 201.3 miles in 1:40.05, 120.08 mph
2. Chuck Parsons (Lola T163-Chevrolet), 60
3. Mario Andretti (McLaren M6B-Ford), 60
4. Dan Gurney (McLeagle-Chevrolet), 60
5. Peter Revson (Lola T163-Chevrolet), 58

Round 11 Results
Texas, No.
1. Bruce McLaren (McLaren M8B-Chevrolet), 70 laps of 3.0 miles = 210.0 miles in 1.54:42.4, 109.854 mph
2. George Eaton (McLaren M12-Chevrolet), 70
3. Jack Brabham (Open Sports Ford), 69
4. Jo Siffert (Porsche 917PA), 69
5. Chuck Parsons (Lola T163-Chevrolet), 67

Final Point Standings 1969
1.	Bruce McLaren	165
2.	Denny Hulme	160
3.	Chuck Parsons	81
4.	Jo Siffert	56
5.	George Eaton	50
6.	Chris Amon	39
7.	Lothar Motschenbacher	35
8.	Tony Dean	31
9.	John Surtees	30
10.	John Cordts	24
11.	Peter Revson	22
	Dan Gurney	22
	Mario Andretti	22
14.	Dick Brown	13
15.	Jack Brabham	12
16.	Leonard Janke	9
	Tom Dutton	9
	Pedro Rodriguez	9
19.	Jacques Couture	8
	Kris Harrison	8
	Andrea de Adamich	8
22.	Oscar Koveleski	7
	Gary Wilson	7
24.	Fred Baker	6
	Dave Causey	6
26.	Rich Galloway	5
27.	Jo Bonnier	4
28.	Joe Leonard	3
	Johnny Servoz-Gavin	3
	Roger McCaig	3
31.	Brooke Doran	2
32.	David Hobbs	1
	Spence Stoddard	1

Note: Split scoring system in Can-Am. Best four finishes in first five races are counted and the best five finishes are counted in the last six races.

1970

Round 1 Results
Mosport, June 14, 1970
1. Dan Gurney (McLaren M8D-Chevrolet), 80 laps of 2.46 miles = 196.72 miles in 1.47:05.6, 110.214 mph (record)
2. Jackie Oliver (Ti22-Chevrolet), 80 laps
3. Denny Hulme (McLaren M8D-Chevrolet), 78
4. Tony Dean (Porsche 908), 73
5. Roger McCaig (McLaren M8C-Chevrolet), 73

Round 2 Results
St. Jovite, June 28, 1970
1. Dan Gurney (McLaren M8D-Chevrolet), 75 laps of 2.65 miles = 198.77 miles in 2.01:45.7, 97.95 mph
2. Lothar Motschenbacher (McLaren M8B-Chevrolet), 75 laps
3. George Eaton (BRM P154-Chevrolet), 73
4. Bob Brown (McLeagle-Chevrolet), 71
5. Roger McCaig (McLaren M8C-Chevrolet), 70

Round 3 Results
Watkins Glen, July 12, 1970
1. Denny Hulme (McLaren M8D-Chevrolet), 87 laps of 2.3 miles = 200.1 miles in 1.41:16, 118.56 mph

2. Jo Siffert (Porsche 917), 87 laps
3. Richard Attwood (Porsche 917), 85
4. Vic Elford (Porsche 917), 85
5. Mario Andretti (Ferrari 512S), 85

Round 4 Results
Edmonton, July 26, 1970
1. Denny Hulme (McLaren M8D-Chevrolet), 80 laps of 2.527 miles = 202.16 miles in 1.54:05.5, 106.4 mph
2. Peter Gethin (McLaren M8D-Chevrolet), 80 laps
3. Lothar Motschenbacher (McLaren M8B-Chevrolet), 79
4. Bob Brown (McLeagle-Chevrolet), 78
5. Dave Causey (Lola T163-Chevrolet), 76

Round 5 Results
Mid-Ohio, August 23, 1970
1. Denny Hulme (McLaren M8D-Chevrolet), 80 laps of 2.4 miles = 199.2 miles in 2.01:03.3, 95.163 mph
2. Peter Revson (Lola T220-Chevrolet), 80 laps
3. Lothar Motschenbacher (McLaren M8B-Chevrolet), 79
4. Chuck Parsons (Lola T163-Chevrolet), 77
5. Gary Wilson (Lola T163-Chevrolet), 76

Round 6 Results
Elkhart Lake, August 30, 1970
1. Peter Gethin (McLaren M8D-Chevrolet), 50 laps of 4.0 miles = 200 miles in 1.54:16.1, 105.016 mph
2. Bob Bondurant (Lola T160-Chevrolet) 49
3. Dave Causey (Lola T163-Chevrolet), 48
4. Gary Wilson (Lola T163-Chevrolet), 48
5. Tony Dean (Porsche 908), 48

Round 7 Results
Road Atlanta, September 9, 1970
1. Tony Dean (Porsche 908), 75 laps of 2.52 miles = 190 miles in 1.40:45, 103.45 mph
2. Dave Causey (Lola T163-Chevrolet), 75 laps
3. Lothar Motschenbacher (McLaren M12-Chevrolet), 72
4. Oscar Koveleski (McLaren M8B-Chevrolet), 72
5. Roger McCaig (McLaren M8C-Chevrolet), 72

Round 8 Results
Donnybrooke, September 27, 1970
1. Denny Hulme (McLaren M8D-Chevrolet), 70 laps of 3.0 miles = 210 miles in 1.47:10.2, 117.57 mph
2. Peter Gethin (McLaren M8D-Chevrolet), 70
3. Peter Revson (Lola T220-Chevrolet), 69
4. Jim Adams (Ferrari 512P), 68
5. Chris Amon (March 707-Chevrolet), not running at finish, fuel pickup, 67

Round 9 Results
Laguna Seca, October 10, 1970
1. Denny Hulme (McLaren M8D-Chevrolet), 80 laps of 1.9 miles = 200 miles in 1.25:58.8, 106.071 mph
2. Jackie Oliver (Ti22 Mk II-Chevrolet), 80 laps
3. Peter Revson (Lola T220-Chevrolet), 79
4. Chris Amon (March 707-Chevrolet), 78
5. Pedro Rodriguez (BRM P154-Chevrolet), 78

Round 10 Results
Riverside, November 1, 1970
1. Denny Hulme (McLaren M8D-Chevrolet), 61 laps of 3.3 miles = 201.3 miles in 1.40:27.4, 120.284 mph
2. Jackie Oliver (Ti22 Mk II-Chevrolet), 61 laps
3. Pedro Rodriguez (BRM P154-Chevrolet), 59
4. Chris Amon (March 707-Chevrolet), 59
5. Lothar Motschenbacher (McLaren M8C-Chevrolet), 59

Final Point Standings 1970
1. Denny Hulme 132
2. Lothar Motschenbacher 65

Final Point Standings 1970 (cont.)
3. Peter Gethin * 56
4. Dave Causey 56
5. Jackie Oliver 45
6. Tony Dean 44
7. Dan Gurney 42
8. Peter Revson 39
9. Bob Brown 35
10. Roger McCaig 34
11. Chris Amon 28
12. Gary Wilson 27
13. Pedro Rodriguez 26
14. Chuck Parsons 19
15. Vic Elford 16
    Oscar Koveleski 16
17. Jo Siffert 15
    Bob Bondurant 15
19. Jim Adams 14
20. George Eaton 12
    Richard Attwood 12
22. Dick Durant * 12
23. Mario Andretti 8
    Tony Adamowicz 8
25. Gijs van Lennep 6
    Gordon Dewar 6
27. Graeme Lawrence * 6
28. Brian Redman 4
29. Leonard Janke 2
    Brooke Doran 2
31. Clif Apel 1
    Ranier Brezinka 1
    Gerard Larrousse 1
    Chuck Frederick 1
    Bob Nagel 1
    Ron Goldleaf 1
    George Drolsom 1
    Peter Gregg 1

* Ties for position resolved by drivers' finishing records throughout the season.
Note: Split scoring system in Can-Am. Best four finishes in first five races are counted and the best four finishes are counted in the last five races.

1971
Round 1 Results
Mosport, June 13, 1971
1. Denny Hulme (McLaren M8F-Chevrolet), 80 laps of 2.46 miles = 196.72 miles in 1.48:15.2, 109.033 mph
2. Peter Revson (McLaren M8F-Chevrolet), 80 laps
3. Lothar Motschenbacher (McLaren M8D-Chevrolet), 79
4. Bob Bondurant (McLaren M8E/D-Chevrolet), 79
5. John Cordts (McLaren M8C-Chevrolet), 78

Round 2 Results
St. Jovite, June 27, 1971
1. Jackie Stewart (Lola T260-Chevrolet), 75 laps of 2.65 miles = 200.75 miles in 1.59:29.1, 100.95 mph
2. Denny Hulme (McLaren M8F-Chevrolet), 75 laps
3. Peter Revson (McLaren M8F-Chevrolet), 74
4. Chuck Parsons (McLaren M8D-Chevrolet), 73
5. Lothar Motschenbacher (McLaren M8D-Chevrolet), 73

Round 3 Results
Road Atlanta, July 11, 1971
1. Peter Revson (McLaren M8F-Chevrolet), 75 laps of 2.52 miles = 189 miles in 1.42:09, 111.17 mph
2. Denny Hulme (McLaren M8F-Chevrolet), 75 laps
3. Lothar Motschenbacher (McLaren M8D-Chevrolet), 74
4. Tony Adamowicz (McLaren M8B-Chevrolet), 72
5. Milt Minter (Porsche 917 PA), 71

Round 4 Results
Watkins Glen, July 25, 1971
1. Peter Revson (McLaren M8F-Chevrolet), 82 laps of 2.428 miles = 199.096 miles in 1.32:54.137, 128.58 mph
2. Denny Hulme (McLaren M8F-Chevrolet), 82 laps
3. Jo Siffert (Porsche 917/10), 80
4. Mario Andretti (Ferrari 712M), 80
5. Tony Adamowicz (McLaren M8B-Chevrolet), 79

Round 5 Results
Mid-Ohio, August 22, 1971
1. Jackie Stewart (Lola T260-Chevrolet), 80 laps of 2.4 miles = 192 miles in 2.00:16.763, 95.777 mph
2. Jo Siffert (Porsche 917/10), 78 laps
3. Tony Adamowicz (McLaren M8B-Chevrolet), 77
4. Herbert Mueller (Ferrari 512M), 76
5. Chuck Parsons (Lola T160-Chevrolet), 75

Round 6 Results
Elkhart Lake, August 29, 1971
1. Peter Revson (McLaren M8F-Chevrolet), 50 laps of 4.0 miles = 200 miles in 1.50:04.758, 109.012 mph
2. Jo Siffert (Porsche 917), 49 laps
3. Vic Elford (McLaren M8E-Chevrolet), 49
4. Lothar Motschenbacher (McLaren M8D-Chevrolet), 49
5. Hiroshi Kazato (Lola T222-Chevrolet), 47

Round 7 Results
Donnybrooke, September 12, 1971
1. Peter Revson (McLaren M8F-Chevrolet), 70 laps of 3.0 miles = 210 miles in 1.45:45.643, 119.137 mph
2. Denny Hulme (McLaren M8F-Chevrolet), 70 laps
3. Gregg Young (McLaren M8E/D-Chevrolet), 69
4. Vic Elford (McLaren M8E-Chevrolet), 69
5. Jo Siffert (Porsche 917/10), 69

Round 8 Results
Edmonton, September 26, 1971
1. Denny Hulme (McLaren M8F-Chevrolet), 80 laps of 2.527 miles = 202.16 miles in 2.07:47.1, 94.922 mph
2. Jackie Stewart (Lola T260-Chevrolet), 80 laps
3. Jackie Oliver (Shadow Mk2-Chevrolet), 78
4. Jo Siffert (Porsche 917/10), 78
5. Milt Minter (Porsche 917 PA), 77

Round 9 Results
Laguna Seca, October 17, 1971
1. Peter Revson (McLaren M8F-Chevrolet), 90 laps of 1.9 miles = 171 miles in 1.33:56.86, 109.210 mph
2. Jackie Stewart (Lola T260-Chevrolet), 90 laps
3. Denny Hulme (McLaren M8F-Chevrolet), 90
4. Brian Redman (BRM P167-Chevrolet), 89
5. Jo Siffert (Porsche 917/10), 88

Round 10 Results
Riverside, October 31, 1971
1. Denny Hulme (McLaren M8F-Chevrolet), 61 laps of 3.3 miles = 201.3 miles in 1.37:36, 123.727 mph
2. Peter Revson (McLaren M8F-Chevrolet), 61 laps
3. Howden Ganley (BRM P167-Chevrolet), 60
4. Sam Posey (McLaren M8E-Chevrolet), 60
5. Chuck Parsons (McLaren M8E/D-Chevrolet), 59

Final Point Standings 1971
1. Peter Revson — 142
2. Denny Hulme — 132
3. Jackie Stewart — 76
4. Jo Siffert — 68
5. Lothar Motschenbacher — 52
6. Milt Minter — 37
7. Tony Adamowicz — 34
8. Chuck Parsons — 30

Final Point Standings 1971 (cont.)
9. Vic Elford — 25
10. Hiroshi Kazato — 19
11. Sam Posey — 16
12. John Cordts * — 14
13. Dave Causey — 14
14. Jackie Oliver — 12
    Gregg Young — 12
    Howden Ganley — 12
17. Tom Dutton * — 12
18. Herbert Mueller — 11
19. Mario Andretti — 10
    Bob Bondurant — 10
    Brian Redman — 10
22. Roger McCaig * — 10
23. Bob Brown — 9
24. Dick Durant * — 7
25. Jim Adams — 7
26. Steve Matchett — 5
27. Andrea de Adamich * — 4
28. Gary Wilson * — 4
29. George Drolsom — 4
30. Charlie Kemp — 3
31. Gijs van Lennep — 2
    George Follmer — 2
33. Bob Nagel — 1
    Jim Butcher — 1

* Ties for position resolved by drivers' finishing records throughout the season.

Note: Split scoring system in Can-Am. Best four finishes in first five races are counted and the best four finishes are counted in the last five races.

1972
Round 1 Results
Mosport June 11, 1972
1. Denny Hulme (McLaren M20), 80 laps of 2.46 miles = 196.8 miles in 1.46:40.0, 110.665 mph
2. Mark Donohue (Porsche 917/10K), 80 laps
3. Peter Revson (McLaren M20), not running at finish, broken crankshaft, 78
4. Milt Minter (Porsche 917/10), 78
5. Peter Gregg (Porsche 917/10), 78

Round 2 Results
Road Atlanta, July 9, 1972
1. George Follmer (Porsche 917/10K), 75 laps of 2.52 miles = 189 miles in 1.39:36.2, 113.96 mph
2. Gregg Young (McLaren M8F), 74 laps
3. Milt Minter (Porsche 917/10), 74
4. Charlie Kemp (Lola T222), 73
5. Peter Gregg (Porsche 917/10), not running at finish, out of fuel, 72

Round 3 Results
Watkins Glen, July 23, 1972
1. Denny Hulme (McLaren M20), 60 laps of 3.377 miles = 202.62 miles in 1.46:14.044, 114.44 mph
2. Peter Revson (McLaren M20), 60 laps
3. Francois Cevert (McLaren M8F), 60
4. David Hobbs (Lola T310), 59
5. George Follmer (Porsche 917/10K), 58

Round 4 Results
Mid-Ohio, August 6, 1972
1. George Follmer (Porsche 917/10K), 80 laps of 2.4 miles = 192 miles in 2.04:2.18, 92.876 mph
2. Jackie Oliver (Shadow Mk3), 80 laps
3. Milt Minter (Porsche 917/10), 77
4. Denny Hulme (McLaren M20), 76
5. Charlie Kemp (Lola T222), 75

Round 5 Results
Elkhart Lake, August 27, 1972
1. George Follmer (Porsche 917/10K), 50 laps of 4.0 miles = 200 miles in 1.48:40.2, 110.426 mph
2. Francois Cevert (McLaren M8F), 49 laps
3. Peter Gregg (Porsche 917/10K), 49
4. Jean Pierre Jarier (Ferrari 712M), 48
5. Gregg Young (McLaren M8F), 48

Round 6 Results
Donnybrooke, September 17, 1972
1. Francois Cevert (McLaren M8F), 70 laps of 3.0 miles = 210 miles in 1.46:43.269, 118.065 mph
2. Milt Minter (Porsche 917/10), 70 laps
3. Jackie Oliver (Shadow Mk3), 70
4. George Follmer (Porsche 917/10K), not running at finish, out of gas, 69
5. John Cordts (McLaren M8D), 68

Round 7 Results
Edmonton, October 1, 1972
1. Mark Donohue (Porsche 917/10K), 80 laps of 2.527 miles = 202.16 miles in 1.50:26.091, 109.870 mph
2. Denny Hulme (McLaren M20), 80 laps
3. George Follmer (Porsche 917/10K), 80
4. Carlos Pace (Shadow Mk3), 78
5. David Hobbs (Lola T310), 78

Round 8 Results
Laguna Seca, October 15, 1972
1. George Follmer (Porsche 917/10K), 90 laps of 1.9 miles = 118 miles in 1.34:18.39, 108.793 mph
2. Mark Donohue (Porsche 917/10K), 90 laps
3. Francois Cevert (McLaren M8F), 88
4. Milt Minter (Porsche 917/10), 86
5. Sam Posey (Porsche 917 PA), 85

Round 9 Results
Riverside, October 29, 1972
1. George Follmer (Porsche 917/10K), 61 laps of 3.3 miles = 201.3 miles in 1.38:31.65, 122.585 mph
2. Peter Revson (McLaren M20), 61 laps
3. Mark Donohue (Porsche 917/10K), 61
4. Jackie Oliver (Shadow Mk3), not running at finish, gearbox, 59
5. David Hobbs (Lola T310), 59

Final Point Standings 1972
1.	George Follmer	130
2.	Denny Hulme *	65
3.	Milt Minter	65
4.	Mark Donohue	62
5.	Francois Cevert	59
6.	Peter Revson	48
7.	David Hobbs	39
8.	Jackie Oliver	37
(9.	Peter Gregg	34
10.	Charlie Kemp	27
11.	Lothar Motschenbacher	26
12.	Gregg Young	23
13.	Jean-Pierre Jarier *	11
14.	Bob Nagel	11
15.	Carlos Pace *	10
16.	Gary Wilson	10
17.	John Cordts	8
	Sam Posey	8
19.	Scooter Patrick *	8
20.	Gordon Dewar	7
21.	Tom Heyser	5
22.	Steve Durst	4
	Ed Felter	4
	Mike Hiss	4
25.	Warren Agor *	4

Final Point Standings 1972 (cont.)
26.	Chuck Parsons	3
	Hans Wiedmer	3
	Willi Kauhsen	3
29.	Tony Dean	2
	Pete Sherman	2
31.	Roger McCaig *	2
32.	Bob Peckham	1

* Ties for position resolved by drivers' finishing records throughout the season.

Note: Split scoring system in Can-Am. Best four finishes in first five races are counted and all four finishes are counted in the remaining races.

1973

Round 1 Results
Mosport, June 10, 1973
1. Charlie Kemp (Porsche 917/10K), 80 laps of 2.46 miles = 196.80 miles in 1.48:38.4, 108.654 mph
2. Hans Wiedmer (Porsche 917/10K), 78 laps
3. Bob Nagel (Lola T260), 77
4. Scooter Patrick (McLaren M8F), 77
5. Steve Durst (Porsche 917/10), 77

Round 2 Results
Road Atlanta, July 7, 1973
1. George Follmer (Porsche 917/10K), 90 laps of 2.46 miles = 226 miles in 1.55:45.4, 117.05 mph
2. Mark Donohue (Porsche 917/30KL), 90 laps
3. Jody Scheckter (Porsche 917/10K), 89
4. David Hobbs (McLaren M20), 87
5. Hurley Haywood (Porsche 917/10K), 85

Round 3 Results
Watkins Glen, July 22, 1973
1. Mark Donohue (Porsche 917/30KL), 60 laps of 3.377 miles = 202.62 miles in 1.43:14.405, 117.757 mph
2. David Hobbs (McLaren M20), 60 laps
3. Jody Scheckter (Porsche 917/10K), 59
4. Charlie Kemp (Porsche 917/10K), 59
5. John Cannon (McLaren M8F), 57

Round 4 Results
Mid-Ohio, August 12, 1973
1. Mark Donohue (Porsche 917/30KL), 84 laps of 2.4 miles = 209.6 miles in 1.58:16.762, 101.409 mph
2. George Follmer (Porsche 917/10K), 84 laps
3. Hurley Haywood (Porsche 917/10K), 80
4. Derek Bell (McLaren M8F), 80
5. Bobby Brown (McLaren M8F), 79

Round 5 Results
Elkhart Lake, August 26, 1973
1. Mark Donohue (Porsche 917/30KL), 25 laps of 4.0 miles = 100 miles in 52:37.2, 114.021 mph
2. Jody Scheckter (Porsche 917/ 10K), 25 laps
3. George Follmer (Porsche 917/10K), 25
4. Scooter Patrick (McLaren M8F), 24
5. Bobby Brown (McLaren M8F), 24

Round 6 Results
Edmonton, September 16, 1973
1. Mark Donohue (Porsche 917/30KL), 50 laps of 2.527 miles = 126.4 miles in 1.09:22.746, 110.867 mph
2. George Follmer (Porsche 917/10K), 50 laps
3. Jackie Oliver (Shadow DN2), 48
4. David Hobbs (McLaren M20), 48
5. Steve Durst (McLaren M8F), 48

Round 7 Results
Laguna Seca, October 14, 1973
1. Mark Donohue (Porsche 917/30KL), 66 laps of 1.9 miles = 125.04 miles in 1.13:05.496, 102.190 mph
2. Jackie Oliver (Shadow DN2), 65 laps
3. Hurley Haywood (Porsche 917/10K), 65
4. Bobby Brown (McLaren M8F), 64
5. Milt Minter (Alfa Romeo T33/3), 64

Round 8 Results
Riverside, October 28, 1973
1. Mark Donohue (Porsche 917/30KL), 49 laps of 2.54 miles = 124.46 miles in 1.02:04.182, 120.311 mph
2. Hurley Haywood (Porsche 917/10K), 49 laps
3. Charlie Kemp (Porsche 917/10K), 48
4. Bob Nagel (Lola T260), 47
5. Milt Minter (Alfa Romeo T33/3), 46

Final Point Standings 1973
1. Mark Donohue — 139
2. George Follmer — 62
3. Hurley Haywood — 47
4. Charlie Kemp — 45
5. Bob Nagel — 44
6. Jody Scheckter — 39
7. David Hobbs — 37
8. Scooter Patrick — 31
9. Jackie Oliver — 30
10. Steve Durst — 29
11. Bobby Brown — 26
12. Milt Minter — 16
13. Hans Wiedmer * — 15
14. Tom Dutton — 15
15. John Cannon — 14
16. Derek Bell * — 10
17. Robert Peckham — 10
18. Danny Hopkins — 8
19. Tom Heyser — 7
20. Gary Wilson — 6
21. Ed Felter * — 4
22. John Cordts — 4
23. Warren Agor * — 3
24. Peter Sherman — 3
25. Peter Gregg * — 2
26. Hanns Muller-Perschl — 2

* Ties for position resolved by drivers' finishing records throughout the season.

1974

Round 1 Results
Mosport, June 16, 1974
1. Jackie Oliver (Shadow DN4), 50 laps of 2.46 miles = 122.95 miles in 1:05.52.2, 112.00 mph
2. George Follmer (Shadow DN4), 50 laps
3. Scooter Patrick (McLaren M20), 49
4. Bob Nagel (Lola T260), 48
5. Lothar Motschenbacher (McLaren M8F), 48

Round 2 Results
Road Atlanta, July 7, 1974
1. Jackie Oliver (Shadow DN4), 44 laps of 2.52 miles = 110.88 miles in 0:57:7.8, 116.90 mph
2. George Follmer (Shadow DN4), 44 laps
3. Lothar Motschenbacher (McLaren M8F), 42
4. Herbert Mueller (Ferrari 512M), 42
5. John Gunn (Lola T260), 41

Round 3 Results
Watkins Glen, July 14, 1974
1. Jackie Oliver (Shadow DN4), 33 laps of 3.377 miles = 111.441 miles in 0:57:15.448, 116.78 mph
2. George Follmer (Shadow DN4), 33 laps
3. Scooter Patrick (McLaren M20), 32
4. Bob Nagel (Lola T260), 31
5. Dick Durant (McLaren M8R), 29

Round 4 Results
Mid-Ohio, August 11, 1974
1. Jackie Oliver (Shadow DN4), 47 laps of 2.4 miles = 112.8 miles in 1.06:17.356, 102.085 mph
2. Brian Redman (Porsche 917/30KL), 47 laps
3. Hurley Haywood (Porsche 917/10), 46
4. Bob Nagel (Lola T260), 44
5. Monte Shelton (McLaren M8F), 44

Round 5 Results
Elkhart Lake, August 25, 1974
1. Scooter Patrick (McLaren M20), 28 laps of 4.0 miles = 112 miles in 1:01.14, 109.344 mph
2. John Cordts (McLaren M8F), 28
3. John Gunn (Lola T260), 28
4. Bob Nagel (Lola T260), 27
5. Gary Wilson (Sting GW1), 27

Final Point Standings 1974
1. Jackie Oliver — 82
2. George Follmer — 45
3. Scooter Patrick — 44
4. Bob Nagel — 40
5. John Gunn — 23
6. Lothar Motschenbacher — 21
7. Dick Durant — 18
8. Dennis Aase — 17
9. Herbert Mueller — 16
10. Brian Redman — 15
    John Cordts — 15
12. Hurley Haywood — 12
13. Monte Shelton — 8
    Gary Wilson — 8
15. David O. Saville-Peck — 7
16. Gene Fisher — 6
    Roy Woods — 6
18. Bill Cuddy — 5
19. Horst Peterman — 4
20. Harry Bytzek — 3
    Arturo Merzario — 3
    Bob Lazier — 3
23. Mike Brockman — 2
24. Tom Butz — 1
    William Morrow — 1

Index

Adam, Hans, 35
Adams, Jim, 139
Adams, Nat, 63
Adams, Nick, 31
Agapiou, Charlie, 19
Agapiou, Kerry, 19
Alexander, Tyler, 58, 71, 75, 88–99, 110, 112, 114, 137
Amon, Chris, 27, 29, 31, 33, 40, 49, 53, 64, 81, 102, 103, 105, 122, 1242
Andretti, Mario, 18, 19, 25, 34, 61, 81, 83, 104, 109, 124, 137, 167–173
Autosport, 11, 37
AutoWeek, 37
Bailey, Roger, 105
Barbour, Mike, 125
Beanland, Colin, 58, 90, 91, 95
Bignotti, George, 77
Bondurant, Bob, 131
Borsari, Giulio, 64
Brabham, 34, 53, 65, 109
Bridgehampton, 169
    1966, 9, 16, 34, 40, 48, 49, 53, 127
    1967, 29, 64, 167, 170
    1968, 11, 71, 79, 80, 82–84, 88
    1969, 99, 107, 147
Broadley, Eric, 53, 55, 131, 138, 168
Brock, Peter, 35
Brown, Dick, 121
Bryant, Peter, 130–133, 137, 139, 141–144, 180, 181
Bucknum, Ron, 27
Burnett, Stan, 34, 87
Caldwell, Alister, 73
Caldwell, Ray, 62
Cannon, John, 27, 81, 84, 87, 124, 173
Causey, Dave, 13
Cevert, Francois, 156, 160
Challman, Bob, 30
Chaparral, 22, 33, 34, 36–47, 77, 119
Chapman, Colin, 30, 91
Chevrolet, 17, 23, 37, 48
Chinetti, Luigi, 64
Chinook, 34
Cooper, 34
Coppock, Gordon, 73, 111
Cordts, John, 103
Courville, Nick de, 86
Cramer, Peyton, 76
Crowe, Barry, 144
Crowe, Gene, 23, 109
DaMota, Candy, 71
Dean, Tony, 125
DeLorean, John, 96
Depew, Ted, 35
Dibley, Hugh, 27, 53
Dioguardi, Nick, 133
Donnybrooke
    1970, 122
    1972, 151, 152, 155
Donohue, Mark, 11–14, 27, 31, 33, 42, 61, 63, 64, 70, 82–84, 99, 144, 151–154, 157–165, 175
Dowd, Al, 76
Durant, Dick, 129, 149
Dutton, Tom, 148
Eaton, George, 122
Edmonton
    1969, 103, 105, 109, 110
    1970, 114
    1972, 145

Elford, Vic, 10, 43, 46, 119, 120, 122–124, 162
Elkhart Lake, 69
    1962, 42
    1967, 52, 57, 62, 168
    1968, 79
    1969, 102, 105, 109, 171
    1970, 114, 125
    1971, 136, 141
    1974, 176
Engines, 16–25
Everett, Graham, 144
Fejer, George, 63
Fejer, Rudy, 63
Ferrari, 24, 34, 61
Florence, Lew, 32
Follmer, George, 11, 27, 31, 61, 83, 87, 122, 124, 151–155, 157–161, 164, 174, 176–179, 182, 183
Ford Motor Company, 31, 34
Ford, Henry, 131
Foyt, A.J., 34
Gardner, Frank, 109
Gates, Don, 43
Genie, 34
Gethin, Peter, 114, 121
Ginther, Richie, 35, 45
Goth, Mike, 147
Grant, Jerry, 16, 27
Greaves, Alec, 69, 75, 137
Gregory, Masten, 27
Guldstrand, Dick, 35
Gurney, Dan, 11, 13, 17, 27, 29, 31, 55, 57, 63, 76, 83, 85, 93, 94, 96, 99, 104, 113, 116, 120, 121, 126–129
Haas, Carl, 64
Hall, Jim, 11, 14, 26, 28, 29, 31, 33, 36–49, 56, 59–61, 63, 64, 70, 77, 79–81, 84, 85, 87, 99, 101, 107, 120, 124, 181
Hall, Sandy, 36
Hamill, Ed, 33, 34
Hansen, Jerry, 34
Harris, Trevor, 12, 141, 177, 178
Hawkins, Paul, 27, 53
Hayes, Charlie, 27, 65
Haywood, Hurley, 165
Heimrath, Ludwig, 27
Herd, Robin, 73, 96, 122
Higgins, Vince, 94
Hill, Graham, 34, 77
Hill, Phil, 9, 29, 31, 40, 41, 48–51, 77
Hobbs, David, 133, 139, 155, 156, 162
Hodges, Jerry, 139, 140
Hofer, Heinz, 165
Holman, John, 167
Huffaker, Joe, 32
Hulme, Denis, 9, 11, 13–15, 31, 46, 57, 58, 60, 63, 65, 67–75, 79, 81, 83–86, 91, 93, 94, 97, 99, 102–104, 110, 113, 114, 116, 119–121, 129, 135, 136, 138, 140, 142, 145, 151, 153, 154, 158–160, 173, 181
Janke, Leonard, 103
Jarier, Jean-Pierre, 174
Jenson, Don, 87
Jones, Parnelli, 18, 27, 31, 56, 61, 63, 64, 76, 77
Kansler, Ernest, 131, 132
Kaser, Jim, 46
Kemp, Charlie, 164
Kerr, Alexander "Skeets", 35
Kerr, Phil, 116
Knutson, Gary, 91, 95
Koveleski, Oscar, 14, 103

Kumnick, Roy, 33
Laguna Seca, 35, 93, 160
    1964, 76
    1966, 30, 33, 37, 51, 64
    1967, 61
    1968, 26, 38, 79, 81, 84, 87
    1969, 15, 103, 104, 128, 131, 171
    1970, 10, 120, 123, 124, 132
    1971, 139, 140
    1972, 12, 153, 162
    1992, 67
Laidlaw, Christine, 14
Lamborghini, 34
Las Vegas, 169
    1966, 51, 76
    1967, 64, 91
    1968, 85
Lawrence, Graeme, 148
Leonard, Joe, 109
Leslie, Ed, 147
Lola, 34, 77
Lotus, 34
Lucas, George, 107
Luginbuhl, Dan, 165
Malone, Malcolm, 52
Martin, Berdie, 165
Masterson, John "Bat", 35
Matich, Frank, 61, 65
Mayer, Teddy, 42, 55, 71, 73, 88, 91–93, 96, 110–117, 123, 127, 137, 144, 156
McCaig, Roger, 139
McHenry, Claire Lyons, 64
McKee, Bob, 34, 61, 65
McKitterick, Skeeter, 86
McLaren, Bruce, 10, 13, 14, 27–29, 31, 33, 34, 40, 46, 49, 52, 53, 55, 57, 58, 60, 63, 67, 69–73, 76, 79, 81, 83, 85, 88–93, 95–97, 99, 101–104, 108–112, 114, 115, 117, 119, 120, 127, 129, 149, 173, 181
McLaren, Patty, 97
Mecom, John, 76, 77
Merlyn, 34
Mid-Ohio, 159–161, 179, 182, 183
    1973, 164
    1974, 175, 176
Minter, Milt, 145, 156
Mirage, 34, 61
Mitchell, Bill, 42
Moody, Holman, 171
Moon, Dean, 133
Morton, John, 147
Mosport, 89, 144, 176, 178, 182
    1966, 31, 54
    1967, 63, 64
    1968, 81
    1969, 103
    1970, 12, 13, 96, 120, 121, 126, 129, 177
    1971, 10, 135, 137
    1972, 152
    1973, 164
Moss, Stirling, 59, 108
Motschenbacher, Lothar, 27, 81, 83
Mt. Tremblant-St. Jovite, 27
Muir, Lee, 84, 112, 144
Muller-Perschl, Hanns, 165
Nagle, Bob, 13, 162
Nethling, Fred, 96
Newman, Paul, 169
Nichols, Don, 12, 122, 124, 137, 139, 141–143, 175, 176, 178, 180, 181
Norris, Ken, 132

Oldsmobille, 23
Oliver, Jackie, 13, 104, 121, 124, 129, 131, 137, 139–141, 154, 155, 160, 175–183
Parks, Mike, 155
Parsons, Chuck, 27, 32, 64, 83, 102–104, 107, 124
Patrick, Scooter, 35, 156, 176
Paul, Jim, 87
Penske, Roger, 31, 70, 76, 82, 89, 152, 154, 157, 158, 160, 175, 176
Polak, Vasek, 145
Porsche, 25, 34, 75
Posey, Sam, 27, 59, 61, 62, 83, 85, 153, 155
Rattenbury, Jim, 125
Rattlesnake Raceway, 139
Redman, Brian, 139, 161, 175, 176, 179, 183
Revson, Peter, 11, 13, 18, 34, 83, 85, 94, 113, 114, 121, 124, 135, 136, 140, 153, 158–160
Reynolds, Billy, 23, 96
Rindt, Jochen, 93
Riverside, 35, 69, 97, 114, 158, 160
   1964, 76
   1966, 29, 33, 64, 168
   1967, 61, 63, 77, 127
   1968, 14, 81, 86
   1969, 10, 94, 106, 107, 109, 116, 131
   1970, 46, 119, 123
   1971, 133, 137, 140, 143, 144
   1972, 132, 153, 154, 155
   1973, 165, 173
Road America, 36, 58
Road Atlanta
   1970, 46, 123, 125
   1972, 152
Rodriguez, Pedro, 30, 103, 122
Rogers, Troy, 47
Scarfiotti, Ludovico, 64, 170
Scheckter, Jody, 164
Schell, Harry, 99
Scott, Skip, 27, 83, 131
Sebring 12-Hour Grand Prix of Endurance
   1965, 37
Seifert, Greg, 165
Shadow, 25
Sharp, Hap, 36, 37, 41, 42, 46, 48
Shelby, Carroll, 18, 19, 76
Shelton, Monte, 154
Shinoda, Larry, 42
Siffert, Jo, 103, 106, 137, 139, 151
Smothers, Dick, 65
Southgate, Tony, 122, 162, 182
Spencer, Doan, 105
Springer, Alwin, 145
St. Jovite, 70, 95, 142, 176
   1965, 90
   1966, 31, 34, 52, 53
   1969, 14, 15, 101, 103, 109, 128, 180
   1970, 113, 120, 121, 124, 131, 177, 181
   1971, 135–138
Stanton, Gene, 34, 35, 49
Stewart, Jackie, 11, 34, 46, 93, 94, 99, 113, 123, 135, 136, 138
Stone, Jimmy, 75
Stroppe, Bill, 77
Surtees, John, 11, 27–29, 31, 33, 52–55, 59, 61, 63, 67, 77, 83, 96, 99, 103, 107, 130, 147
Taylor, Cary, 75
Terry, Len, 86
Texas World Speedway, 109
   1969, 167
The Unfair Advantage, 99, 160
Timanus, John, 46

Titus, Jerry, 83
Traco, 20
Truesdale, Larry, 143
Underwood, Mike, 91
United States Road Racing Championship
   1964, 37
Unser, Bobby Jr., 86
Vintage Motorsport, 37
Waters, Doug, 33
Watkins Glen, 9, 159, 183
   1965, 39
   1970, 46, 123
   1971, 167, 172
   1972, 152
   1973, 164
   1974, 174, 178
   1990, 67
Webster, 34
Weslake Engineering, 55
Wietzes, Eppie, 27, 63
Williams, Ben, 143
Williams, Jonathan, 64
Willow Springs, 131
Wilson, Gary, 96, 139
Winchell, Frank, 42
Wolverine, 34
Woodard, Woody, 165
Wyer, John, 131
York, David, 131

Models
Alfa Romeo T33/4, 156
BRM
   P154, 122, 125
   P167, 139
Bryant
   Mark 2, 131
   Mark 3, 131
   Ti22, 12, 13, 104, 121, 129, 131–133, 139, 141, 180
Burnett Mark 3, 87
Caldwell
   D7, 61
   D7A, 59, 62
   D7B, 62
Challman Cherokee Mark 1, 30
Chaparral
   2, 39
   2A, 41–43
   2C, 45
   2E, 9, 28, 29, 31, 33, 40–42, 48–51, 54, 80
   2G, 11, 14, 26, 36, 38, 42, 56, 59–61, 79–81, 85, 87
   2H, 46, 55, 103, 107
   2J, 10, 37, 43, 44, 46, 47, 116, 119, 120, 123, 124
   M12, 147
Chinook Mark 1, 63
Cooper, 109
   F1, 89
Ferrari
   512M, 155
   612P, 81, 105
   712M, 157, 169, 172
   Dino, 30
   P3, 64
   P4, 64
Ford, 109
   G7A, 124
   GT40, 63
Genie
   Mark 10, 32
   Mark 8, 32

Hamill
   SR2, 33
   SR3, 33
Hodges LSR, 140
Hodges/McKee, 139
Lola
   T160, 62, 81, 83, 85
   T162, 154
   T163, 13, 104, 107, 129
   T220, 121, 124
   T260, 135–138, 162
   T310, 155, 156
   T70 Mark IIIb Roadster, 54
   T70, 13, 16, 27–29, 31, 33, 52, 53, 57, 61, 64, 83, 87, 127, 168
   T79, 57
Lotus
   19, 32
   30, 30, 35
March 707, 122, 124
Matich SR3R, 65
McKee
   Mark 14, 109
   Mark 6, 65
   Mark 7, 65
McLaren
   M12, 103, 139, 148
   M16, 111
   M19, 111
   M1A, 147
   M1B, 28, 29, 31, 33, 53, 81, 84, 87, 90
   M1C, 62, 64, 71, 87
   M20, 74, 111, 152–154, 158, 160–162, 172, 173, 176
   M21, 111
   M6, 73
   M6A, 57, 58, 60, 61, 91, 92, 99
   M6B, 14, 81–83, 85, 87, 104, 119, 127, 128, 148, 168, 171
   M6GT, 96
   M8A, 14, 71, 79, 80, 83, 85, 86, 88, 92, 136, 149
   M8B, 14, 72, 81, 93, 94, 97, 101–103, 105, 110, 116, 128, 129, 146
   M8C, 139
   M8D, 13, 113, 121, 126
   M8F, 135, 136, 138, 156
   M8R, 149
   M8B, 104
Nethercutt Mirage, 35
PAM, 35
Porsche, 157–616
   908, 125
   917, 16, 139, 145, 154
   917/10K, 12, 151, 153, 158, 161, 163, 164
   917/30, 13, 161, 163, 164, 175, 176
   917PA Spyder, 106
   917PA, 104, 153
   Panzer 917/10K, 157
   SP20, 165
Rattenbury Mark 4, 125
Shadow, 139, 141–144, 156, 177–182
   DN2, 162, 182, 183
   DN4, 175, 176, 178, 179, 182
   Mark II, 140, 141
   Mark III, 144, 155
   Mark, 137
   Tiny Tire AVS, 12, 176, 177
Stanton, 34
Terry T10, 86
Troutman and Barnes Type 1, 43
Wolverine, 34